AUTHENTIC TRANSCRIPTIONS
WITH NOTES AND TABLATURE

sublime
robbin' the hood

Music transcriptions by Paul Pappas

ISBN 978-1-4234-8122-5

HAL•LEONARD®
CORPORATION

7777 W. BLEUMOUND RD. P.O. BOX 13819 MILWAUKEE, WI 53213

Visit Hal Leonard Online at
www.halleonard.com

Waiting for Bud

Words and Music by Brad Nowell

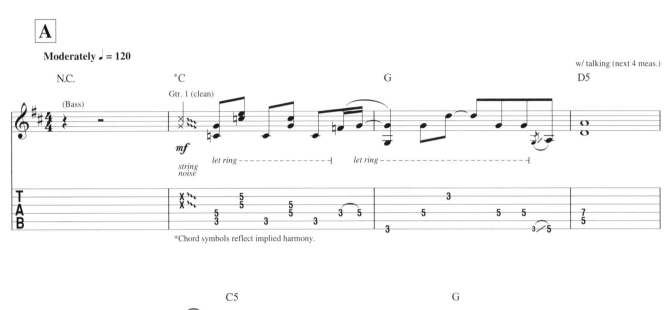

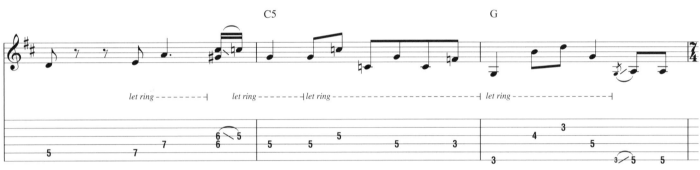

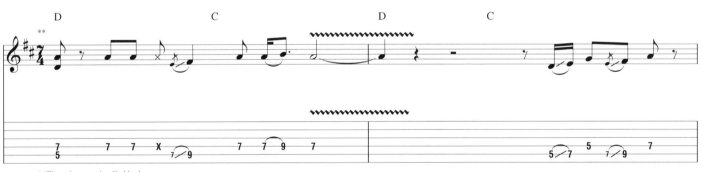

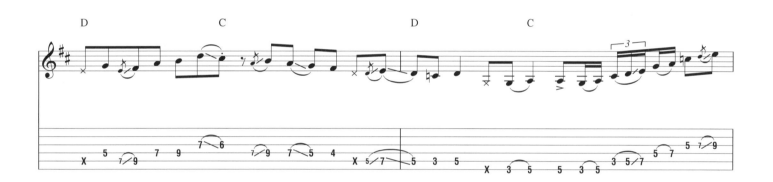

Begin fade

w/ talking (till end)   *Fade out*

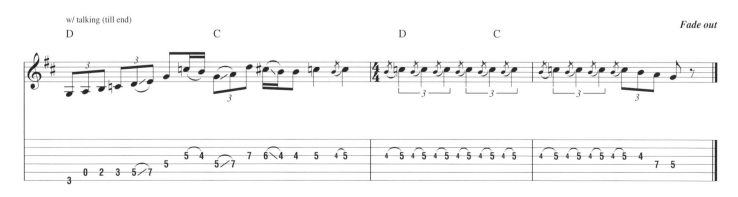

Pool Shark

Words and Music by Brad Nowell

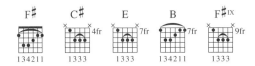

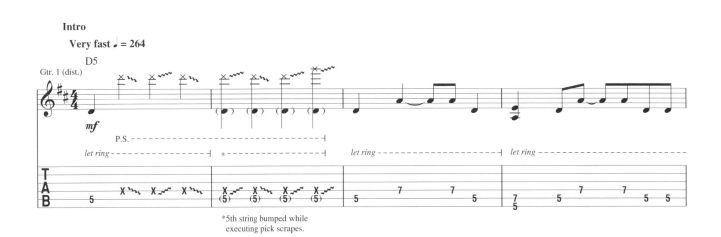

*5th string bumped while
executing pick scrapes.

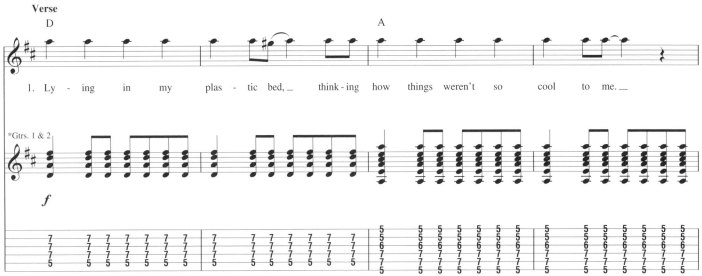

*Gtr. 2 (dist.)
Composite arrangement

My ba - by likes to shoot pool. _ I like ly - ing na - ked in my bed - room.

(Gtr. 2, cont. in slashes)

Ty - ing on _ that di - no - saur _ to - night, _ it used to be _ so cool.

(cont. in notation)

let ring

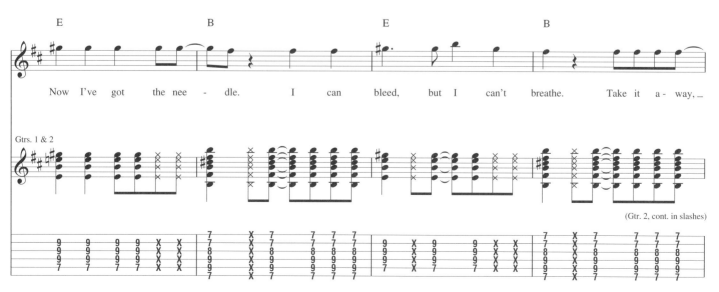

Now I've got the nee - dle. I can bleed, but I can't breathe. Take it a - way, _

(Gtr. 2, cont. in slashes)

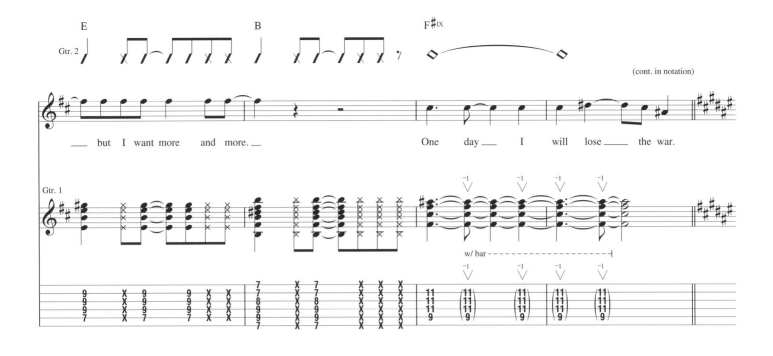

_____ but I want more and more. _____ One day _____ I will lose _____ the war.

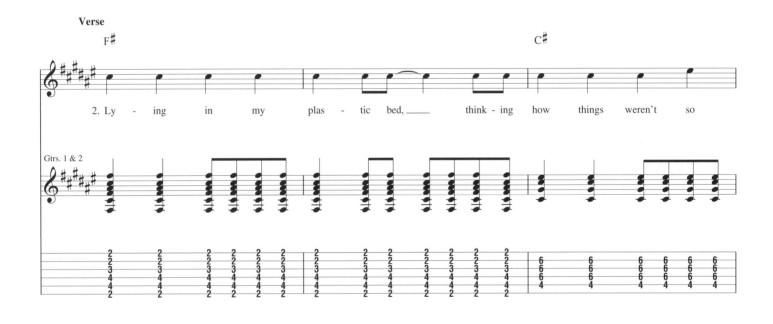

Verse

2. Ly - ing in my plas - tic bed, _____ think - ing how things weren't so

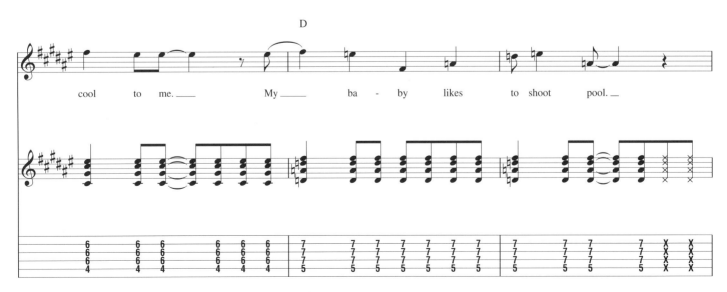

cool to me. _____ My _____ ba - by likes to shoot pool. _____

7

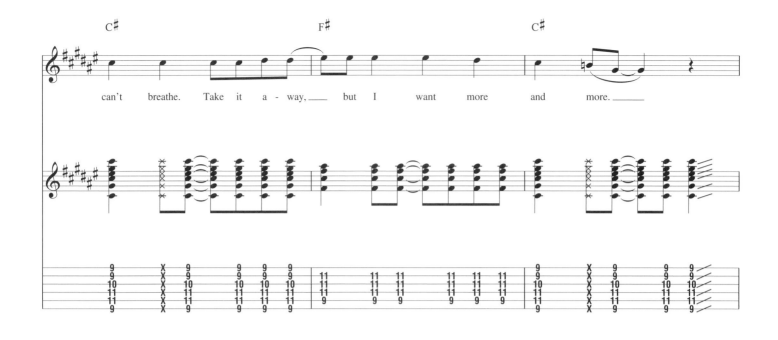

can't breathe. Take it a - way, ___ but I want more and more. ___

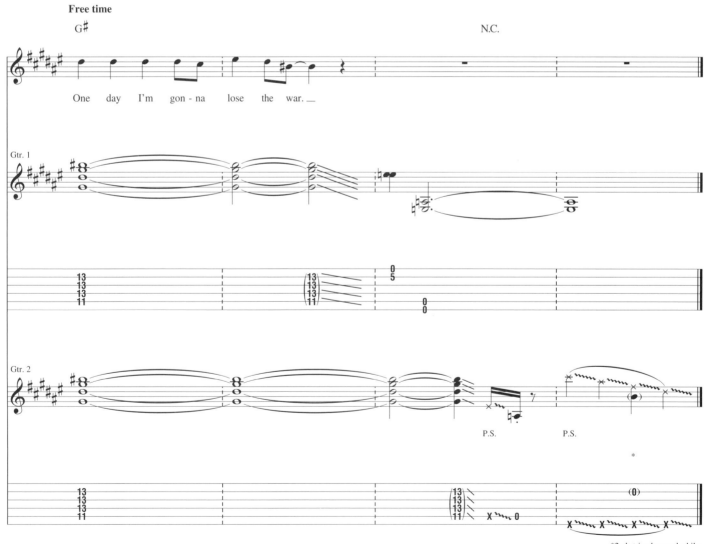

Free time

One day I'm gon - na lose the war. ___

Gtr. 1

Gtr. 2

P.S.   P.S.

*2nd string bumped while
executing pick scrape.

Steppin' Razor

Words and Music by Joe Higgs

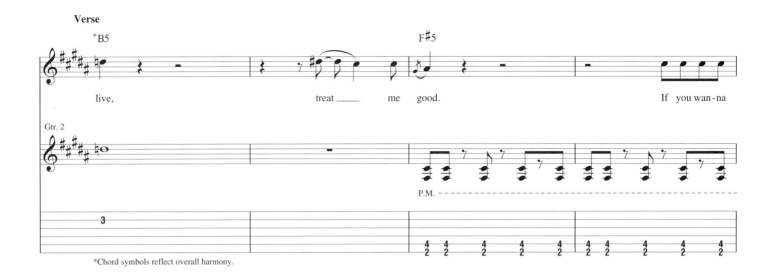

*Chord symbols reflect overall harmony.

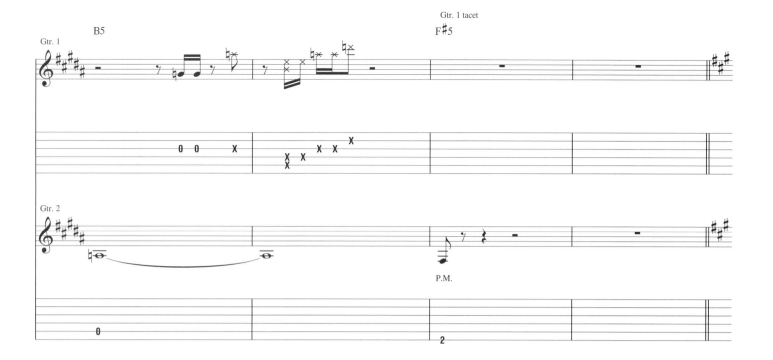

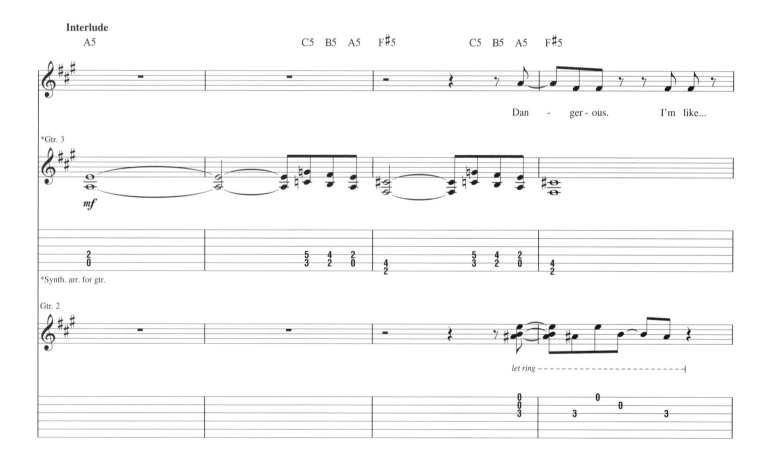

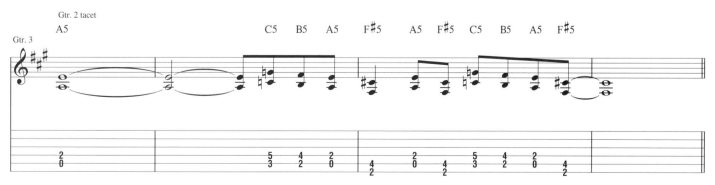

Guitar Solo

Gtr. 3 tacet

N.C.

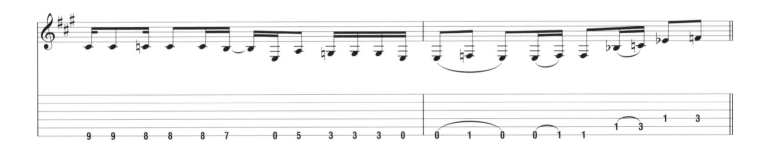

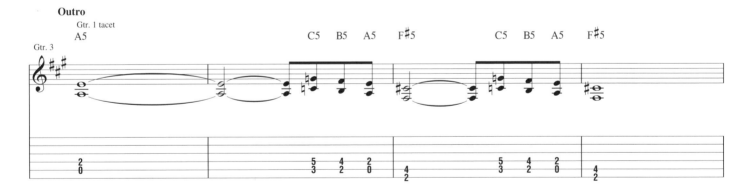

Outro

Gtr. 1 tacet

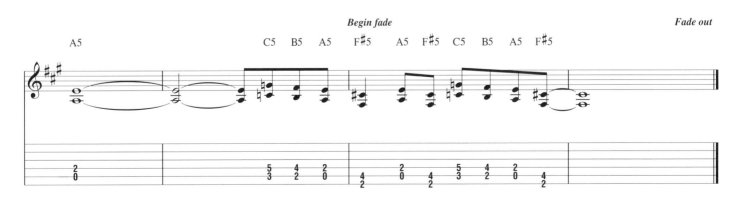

Greatest-Hits

Words and Music by Brad Nowell

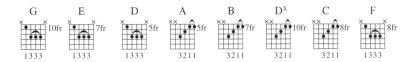

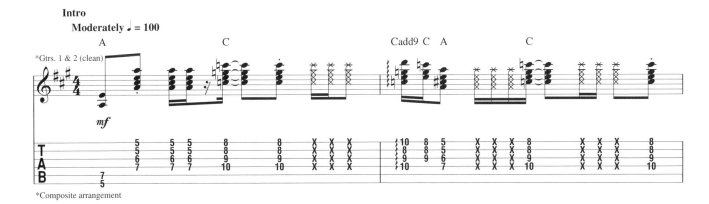

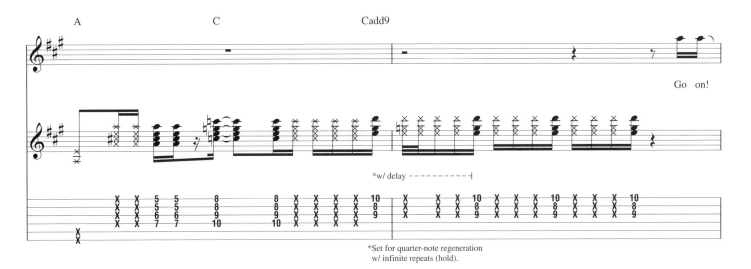

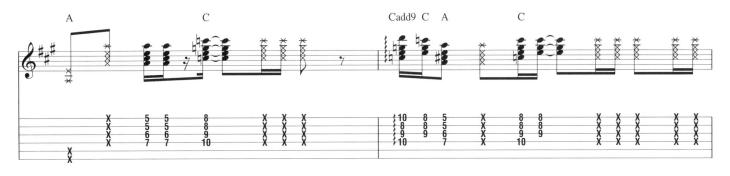

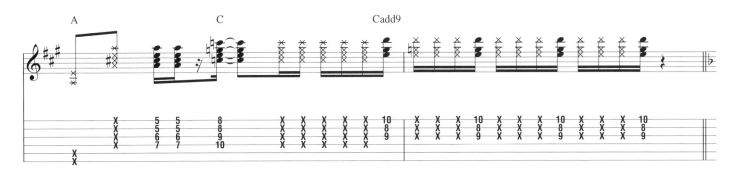

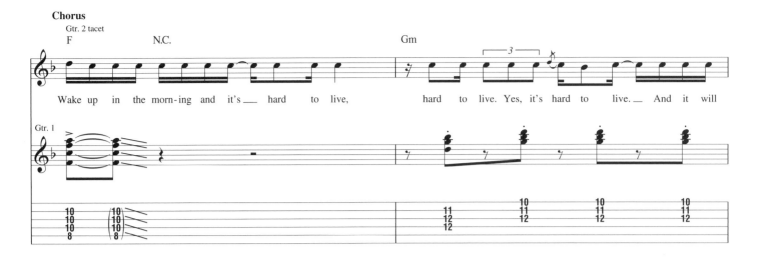

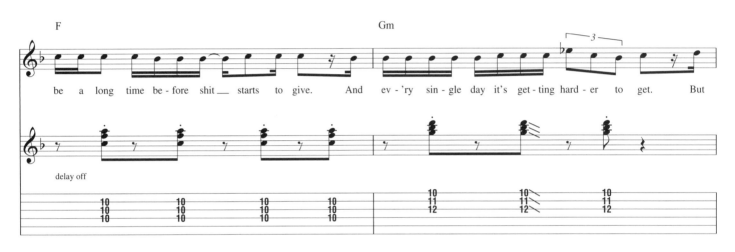

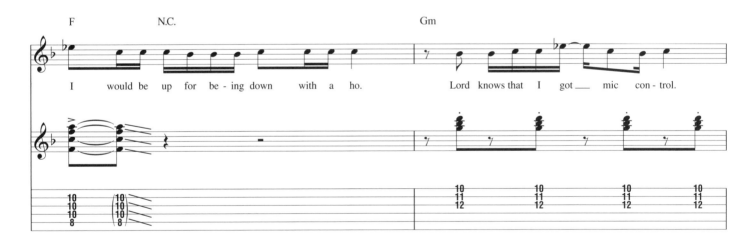

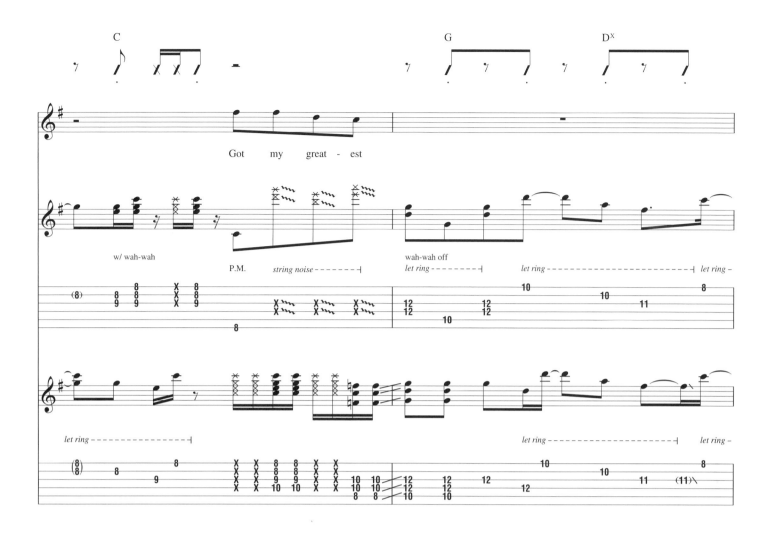

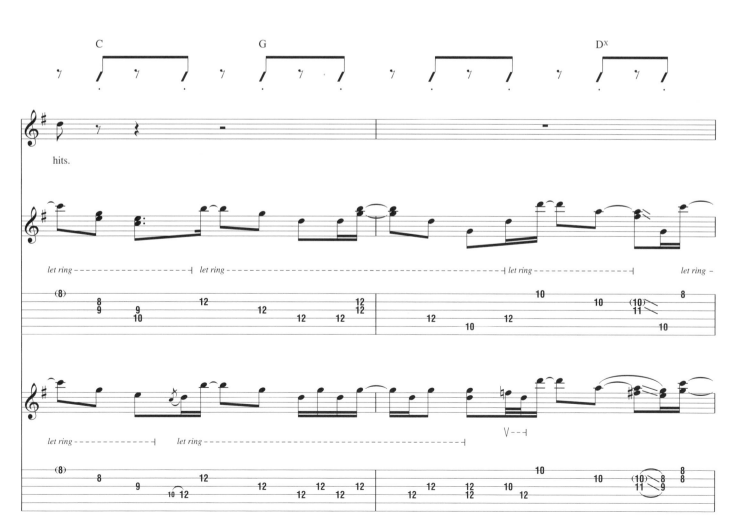

Verse

Got my cig-a-rette _ and I think how Bert Su-san-ka made _ me drink. _

Load the box _ and I'll pump the shit.

Interlude

Chorus

Gtrs. 1, 3 & 4 tacet

Wake up in the morn-ing and it's __ hard to live, and hard to live. Yes, it's hard to live. __ And it will

*w/ delay set for quarter-note regeneration
w/ 1 repeat (next 4 meas.)

be a long time be-fore shit __ starts to give. And ev-'ry sin-gle day it's get-ting hard-er to get. But

I would be up for be-ing down with a ho. Lord knows that I got __ mic con-trol.

Gtr. 1

Do you got mic con-trol? __ You no-tice your style is, well, o-rig-i-nal. 3. This __

(cont. in slashes)

*w/ delay set for quarter-note regeneration
w/ infinite repeats (hold).

23

Verse

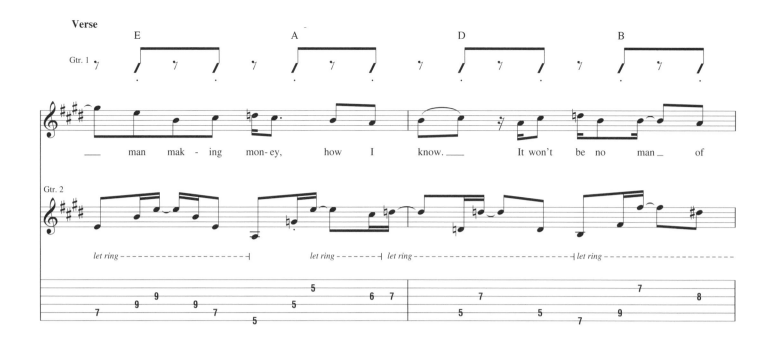

man mak - ing mon-ey, how I know. ___ It won't be no man ___ of

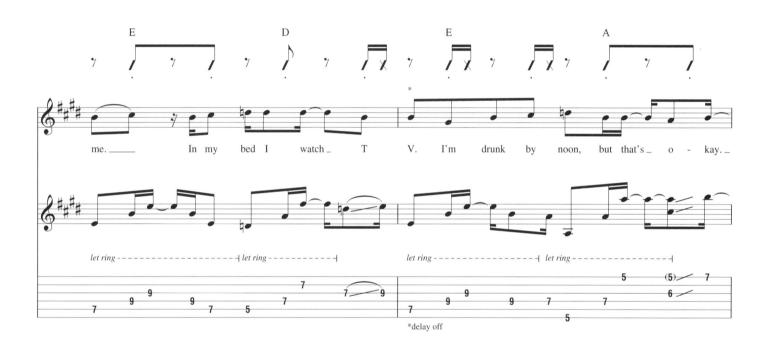

me. ___ In my bed I watch _ T V. I'm drunk by noon, but that's _ o - kay. ___

*delay off

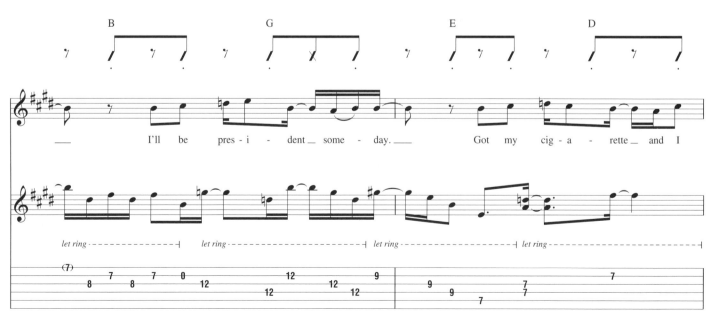

___ I'll be pres - i - dent _ some - day. Got my cig - a - rette _ and I

E   A   B   D   E

(cont. in notation)

think how Burt Su - san - ka made __ me drink. __ Load the box __ and I'll pump the shit.

let ring - - - - - - - - - - - - - let ring - - - - - - - - - - - - - let ring - - - - - - - - - - - - -

*w/ delay set for quarter-note regeneration w/ infinite repeats (hold).

Outro
Double-time feel
Gtr. 2 tacet

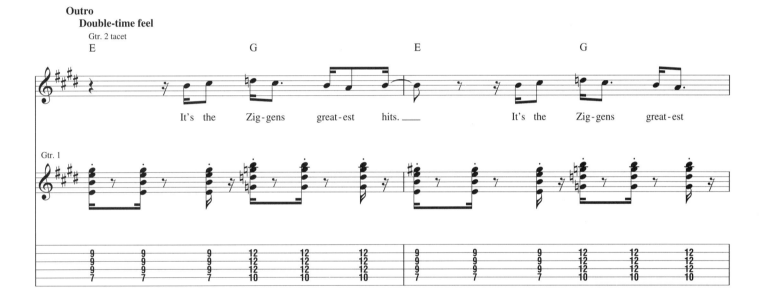

E   G   E   G

It's the Zig - gens great - est hits. __ It's the Zig - gens great - est

Gtr. 1

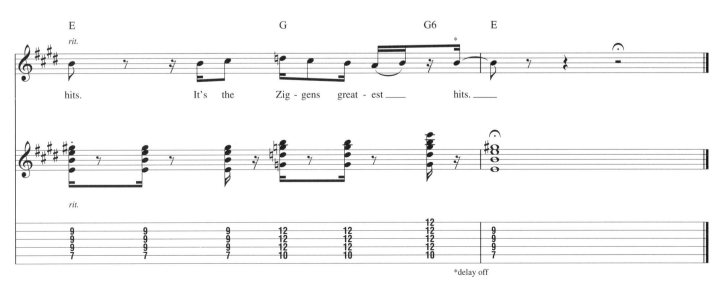

E   G   G6   E

hits. It's the Zig - gens great - est __ hits. __

rit.

*delay off

Saw Red

Words and Music by Brad Nowell and Barrington Levy

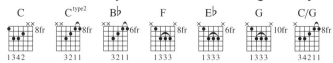

Intro

Moderately slow ♩ = 96

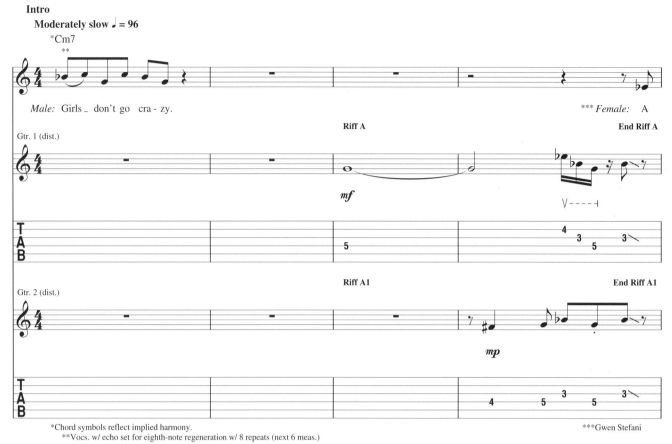

Male: Girls _ don't go cra - zy.

***Female: A

*Chord symbols reflect implied harmony.
**Vocs. w/ echo set for eighth-note regeneration w/ 8 repeats (next 6 meas.)

***Gwen Stefani

Faster ♩ = 220

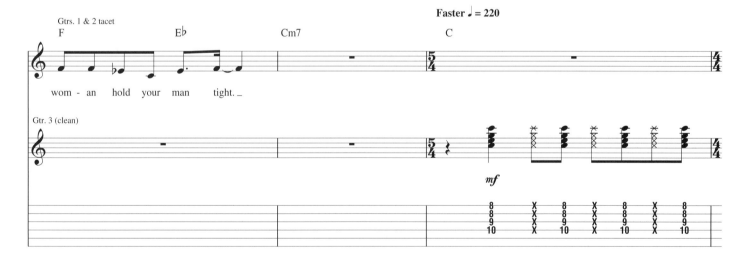

wom - an hold your man tight. _

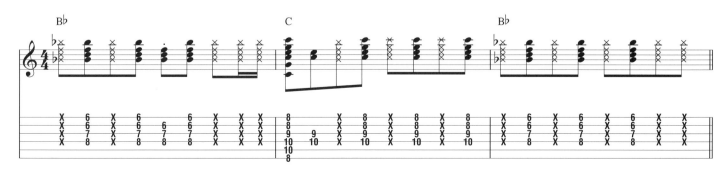

Verse

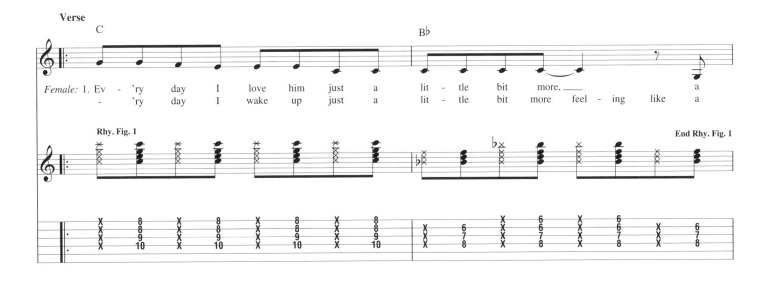

Female: 1. Ev - 'ry day I love him just a lit - tle bit more, _____ a a
     - 'ry day I wake up just a lit - tle bit more feel - ing like a

1st time, Gtr. 3: w/ Rhy Fig. 1 (1 1/2 times)
2nd time, Gtr. 3: w/ Rhy. Fig. 1 (7 times)

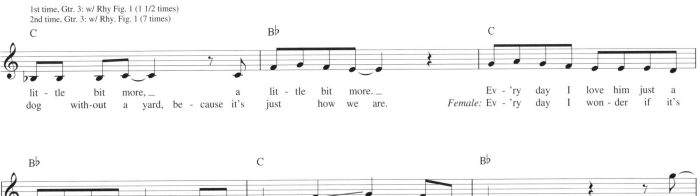

lit - tle bit more, _____ a lit - tle bit more. _____ Ev - 'ry day I love him just a
dog with-out a yard, be - cause it's just how we are. Female: Ev - 'ry day I won - der if it's

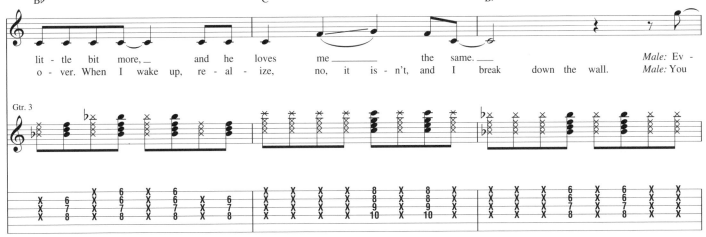

lit - tle bit more, _____ and he loves me _____ the same. _____ Male: Ev -
o - ver. When I wake up, re - al - ize, no, it is - n't, and I break down the wall. Male: You

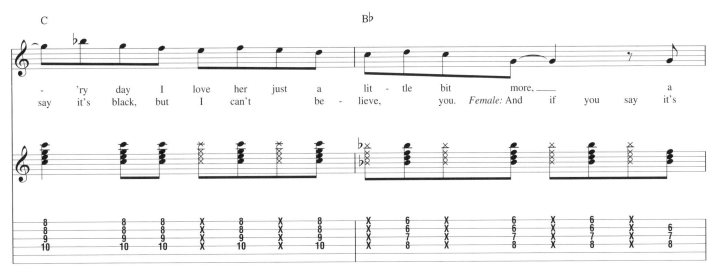

- 'ry day I love her just a lit - tle bit more, _____ a
say it's black, but I can't be - lieve, you. Female: And if you say it's

1st time, Gtr. 3: w/ Rhy. Fig. 1 (3 times)

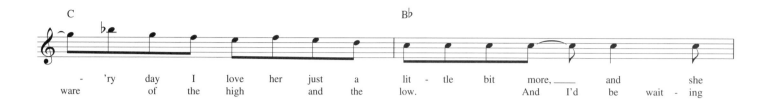

lit - tle bit more, _____ a lit - tle bit more. _____ Ev -
white, you say I'm try - ing to de - ceive you. *Male:* But, ba - by, I'm a -

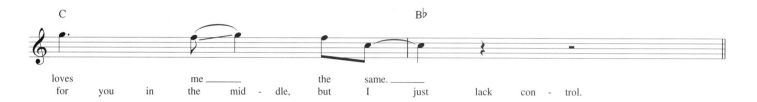

-'ry day I love her just a lit - tle bit more, _____ and she
ware of the high and the low. And I'd be wait - ing

loves you in me _____ the same. _____
for you in the mid - dle, but I just lack con - trol.

Chorus
Double-time feel

Male: 1. Ba - by, if you wan - na get on. _____ *Female:* Oh, _____ ba - by, if you wan - na get off. _____
Male: 2. Ba - by, if you wan - na get low. _____ *Female:* Oh, _____ ba - by, if you wan - na get high. _____

*Gtrs. 1 & 2

*Composite arrangement

End double-time feel

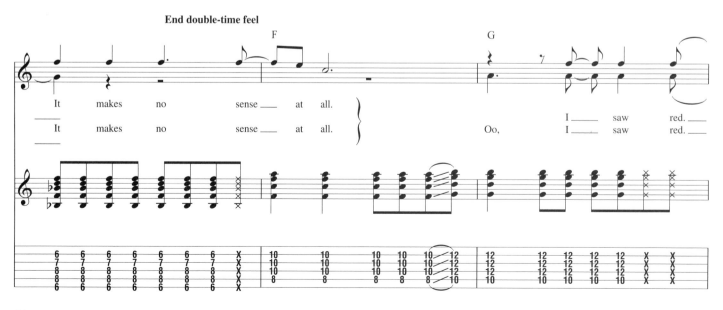

It makes no sense _____ at all.
_____ It makes no sense _____ at all. Oo, I _____ saw red. _____
I _____ saw red. _____

28

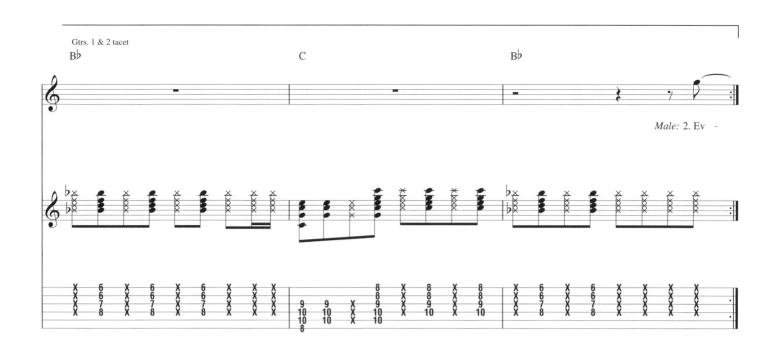

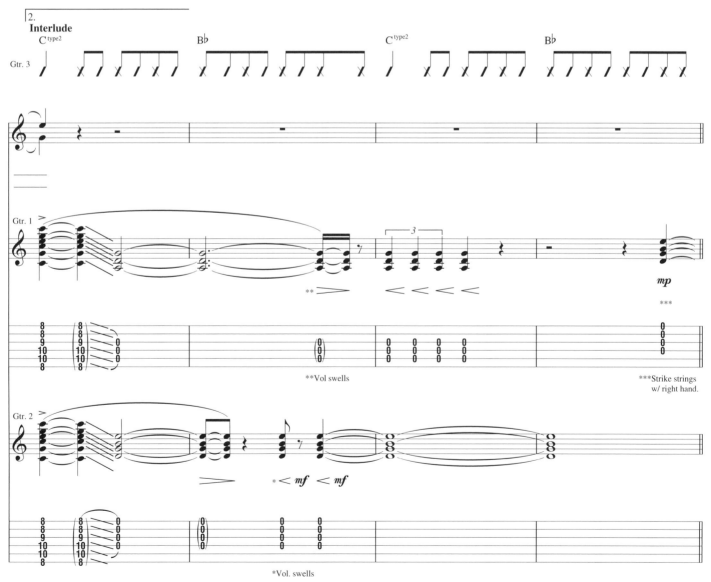

Work That We Do

Words and Music by Brad Nowell

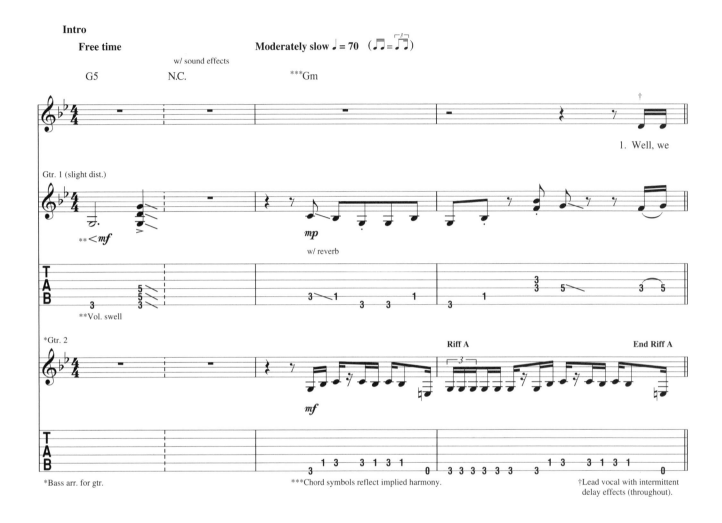

*Bass arr. for gtr. ***Chord symbols reflect implied harmony. †Lead vocal with intermittent delay effects (throughout).

seen it all.___ The lies _____ won't get you.

I've got four-teen miles to go.___ I've got rhy-thm com-in' since I've got the sto. But I

won't wan-na come a-round__ our__ love. So why?

If you are rich, I'm gon-na hang you on the wall and I'm-a find you. And when I

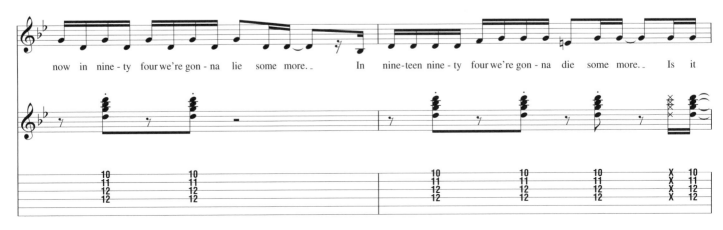

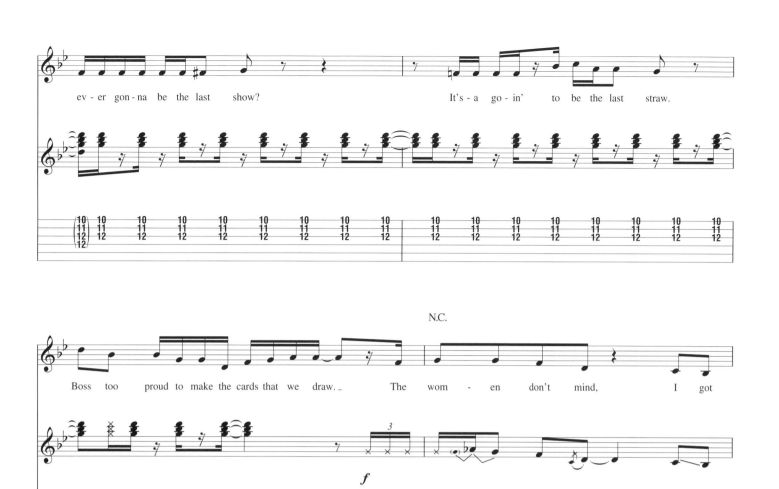

ev - er gon - na be the last show? It's - a go - in' to be the last straw.

N.C.

Boss too proud to make the cards that we draw. _ The wom - en don't mind, I got

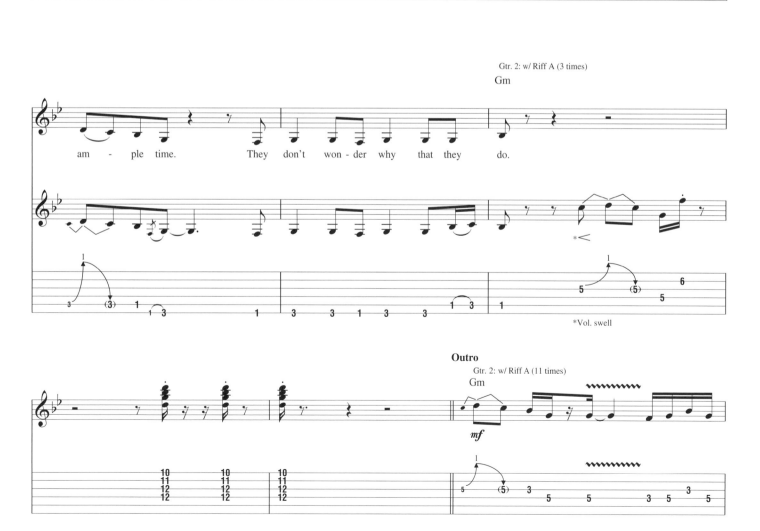

Gtr. 2: w/ Riff A (3 times)
Gm

am - ple time. They don't won - der why that they do.

*Vol. swell

Outro
Gtr. 2: w/ Riff A (11 times)
Gm

Your man.

Long time for me.   Lov - er won't go, ____ what the love won't go. ____

Why don't you wan - na work a - while?   Why don't you wan - na make the oth - er   side?

May - be wan - na ____ be a heav - y load.   Oh.   We are two, ____ us and me. ____

Lincoln Highway Dub

Words and Music by Brad Nowell

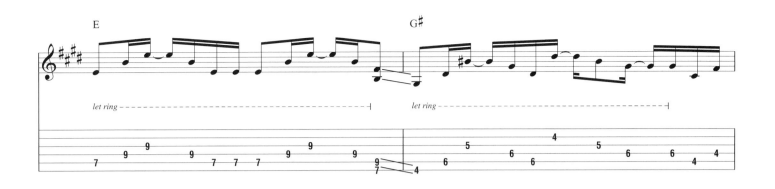

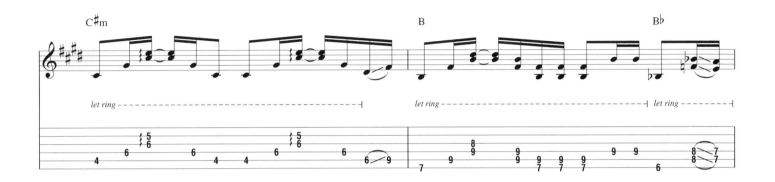

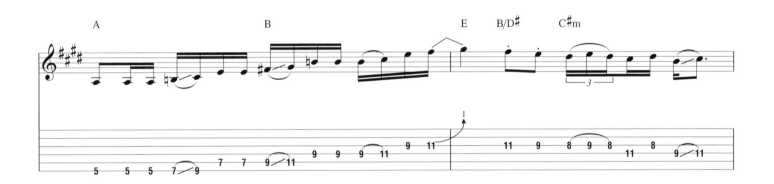

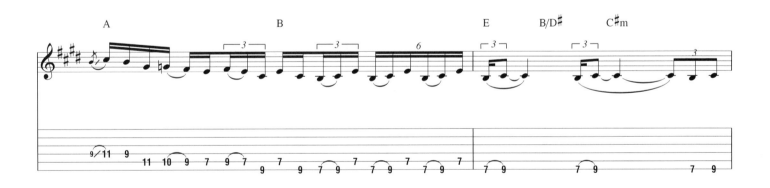

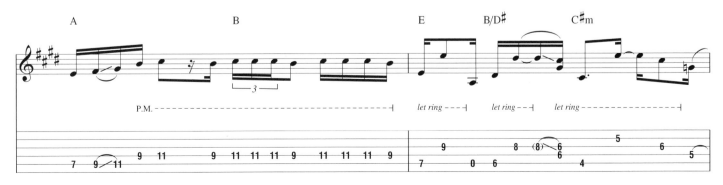

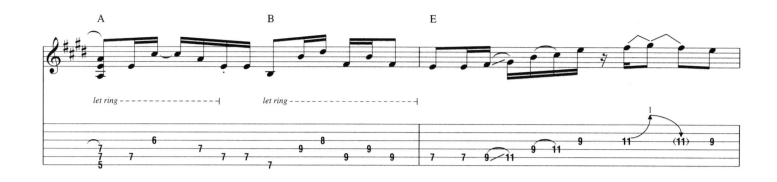

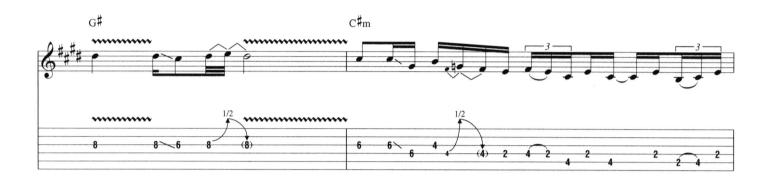

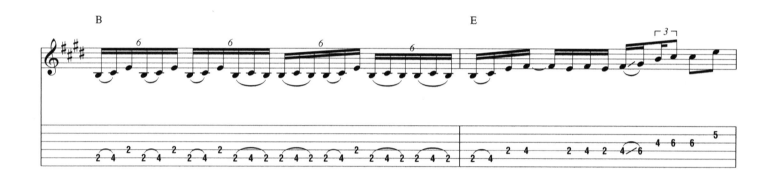

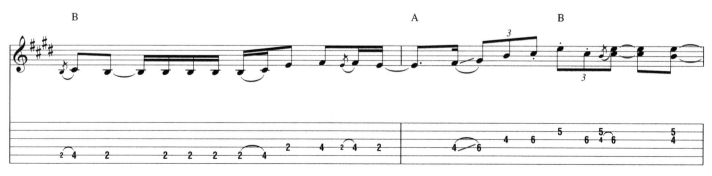

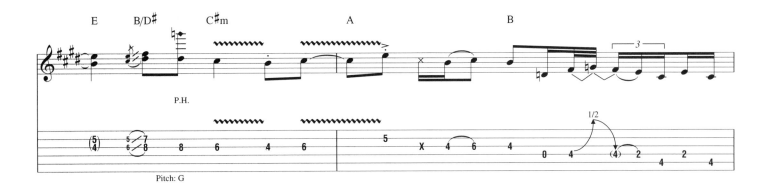

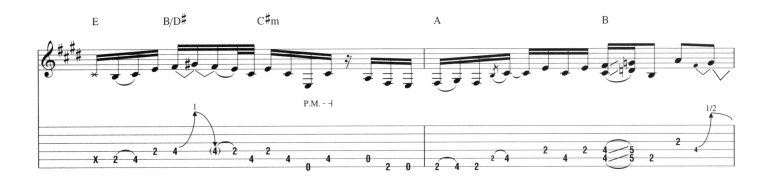

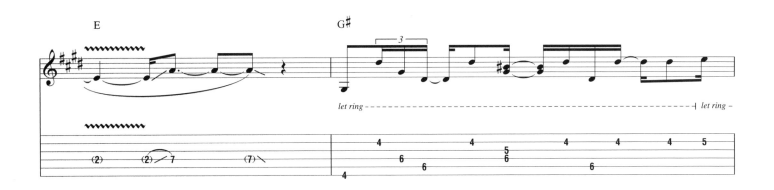

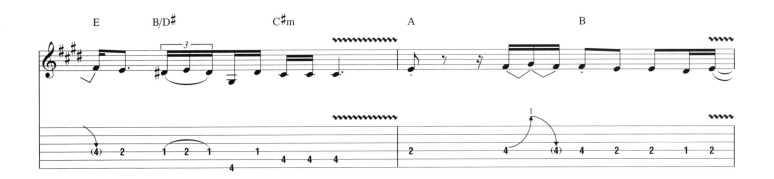

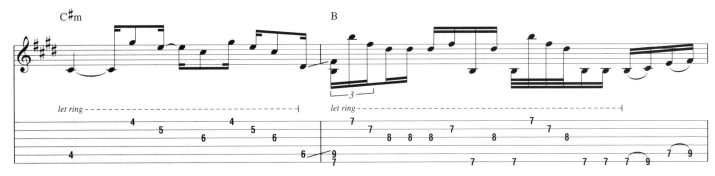

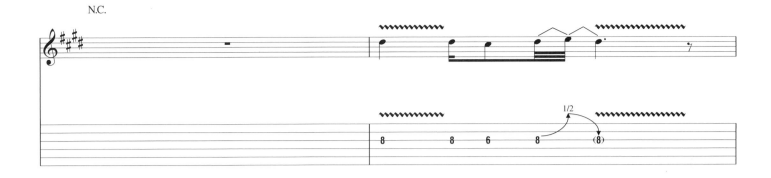

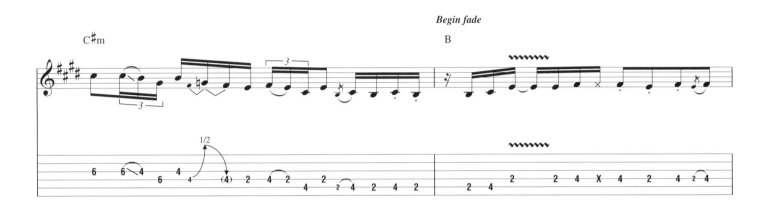

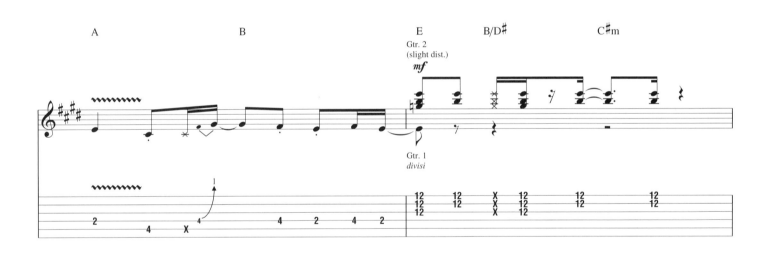

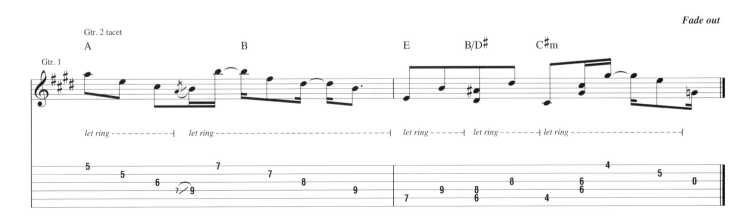

Pool Shark (Acoustic)

Words and Music by Brad Nowell

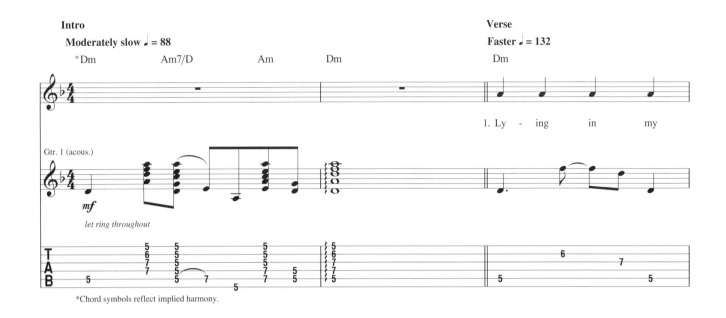

*Chord symbols reflect implied harmony.

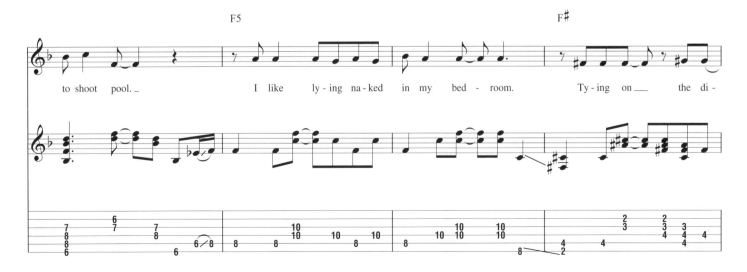

44

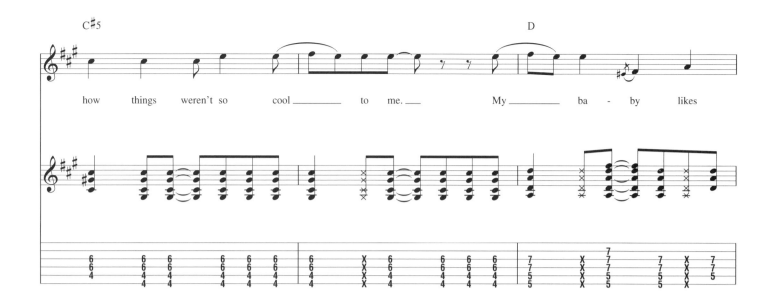

so cool. Now I've got the nee - dle and I can shake,

but I can't breathe. I take it a - way, but I want more and more.

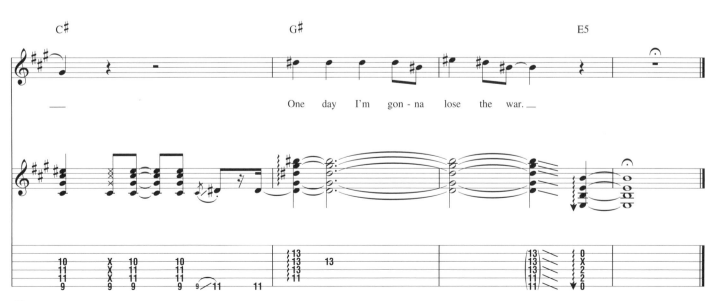

One day I'm gon - na lose the war.

STP

Words and Music by Brad Nowell

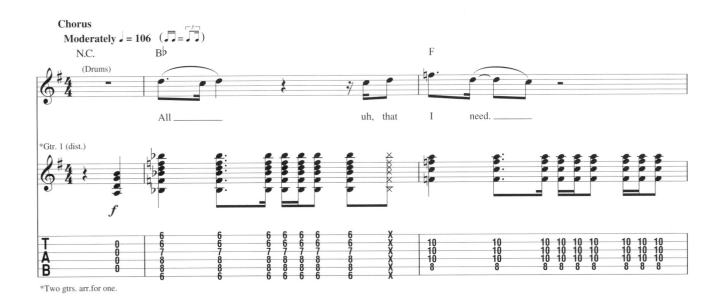

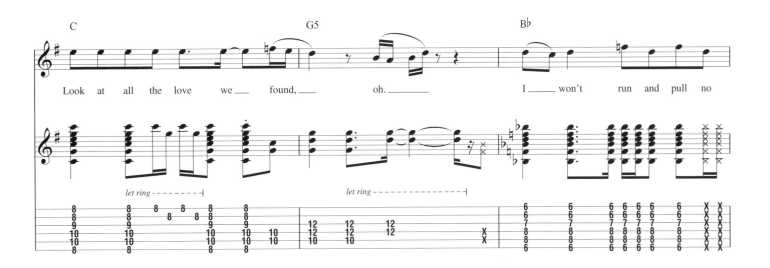

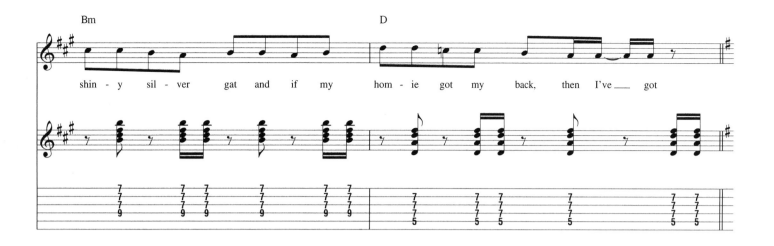

shin - y sil - ver gat and if my hom - ie got my back, then I've __ got

Chorus

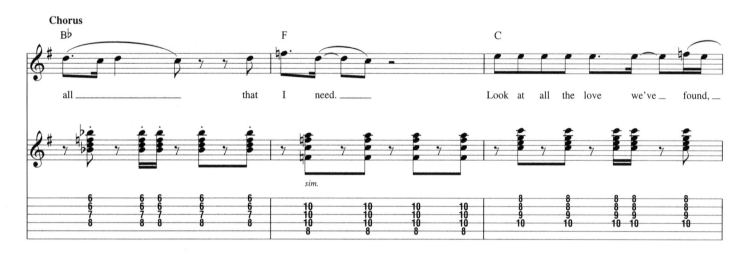

all _____ that I need. _____ Look at all the love we've __ found, __

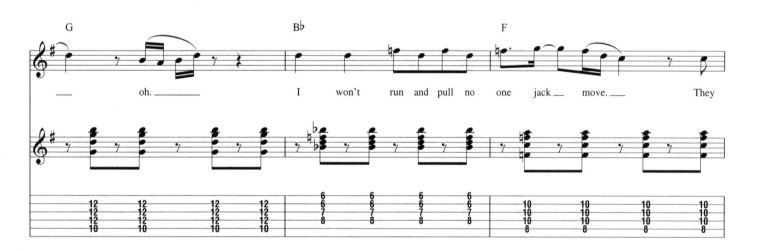

__ oh. _____ I won't run and pull no one jack __ move. ___ They

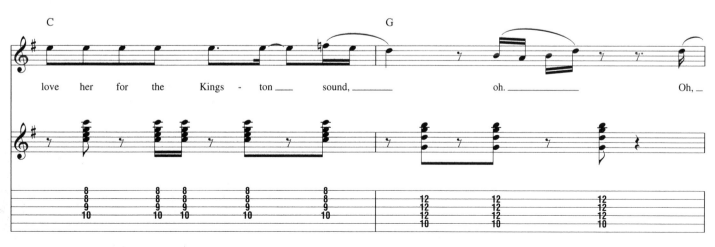

love her for the Kings - ton __ sound, _____ oh. _____ Oh, __

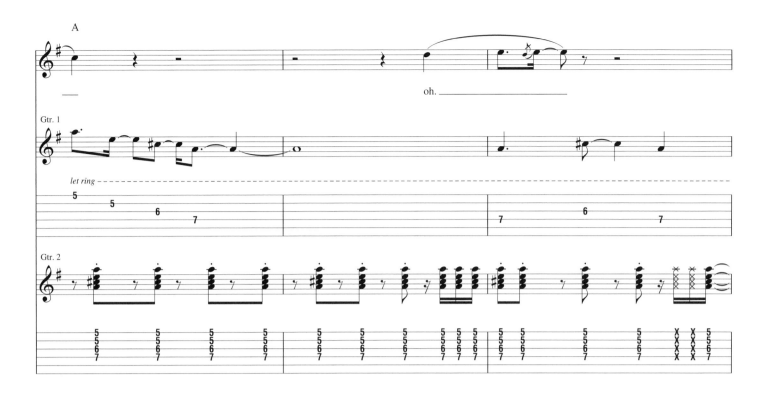

A

oh. _____

Gtr. 1

let ring - - - - - - - - - - -

Gtr. 2

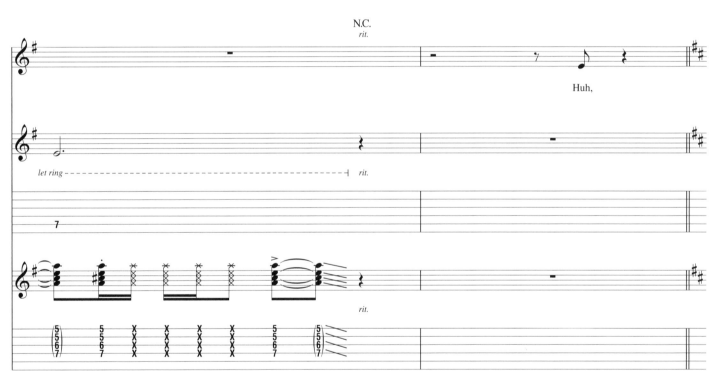

N.C.
rit.

Huh,

let ring - rit.

rit.

Bridge
Slightly faster ♩ = 116

Gtr. 1 tacet

*D   Bm   G

I won't slip, and I won't trip. ___ Send Matt Var - gas

Gtr. 2

let ring - - - - - - - - - - -   let ring - - - - - - - - -   let ring - - - - - - - - -

*Chord symbols reflect implied harmony.

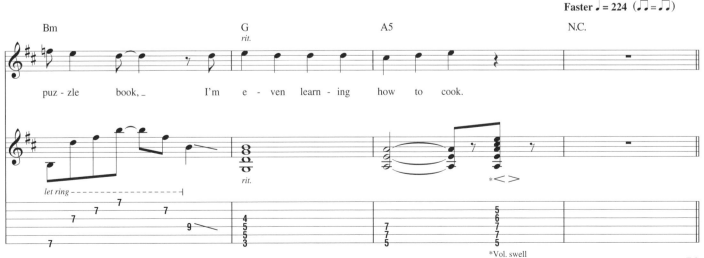

Verse

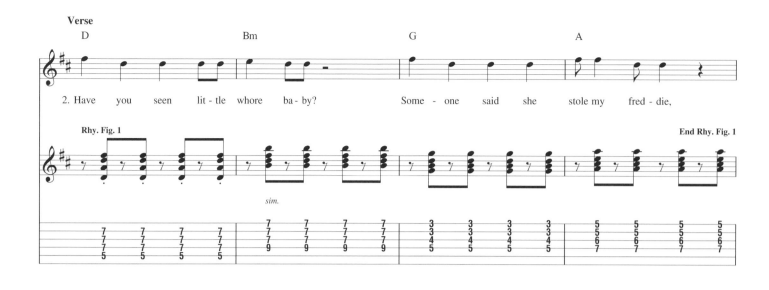

2. Have you seen lit-tle whore ba-by? Some-one said she stole my fred-die,

Gtr. 2: w/ Rhy. Fig. 1 (4 times)

and then she made off with my last clean rig. I'm gon-na kill that

fuck-ing bitch pig. So what? Out-ta my, out-ta my, out-ta my, out-ta my,

out-ta my se-cret pad_____ 'cause I know you're talk-ing a-bout me, ba-by.

Hard to live 'cause I don't want no-bod-y take o-ver, no mon-ey down. My

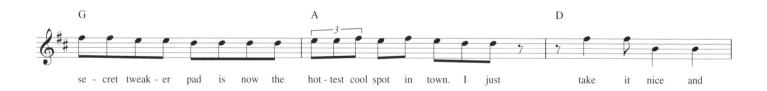

se-cret tweak-er pad is now the hot-test cool spot in town. I just take it nice and

eas-y. Don't want no sher-iff break-ing down the door to raid me 'cause

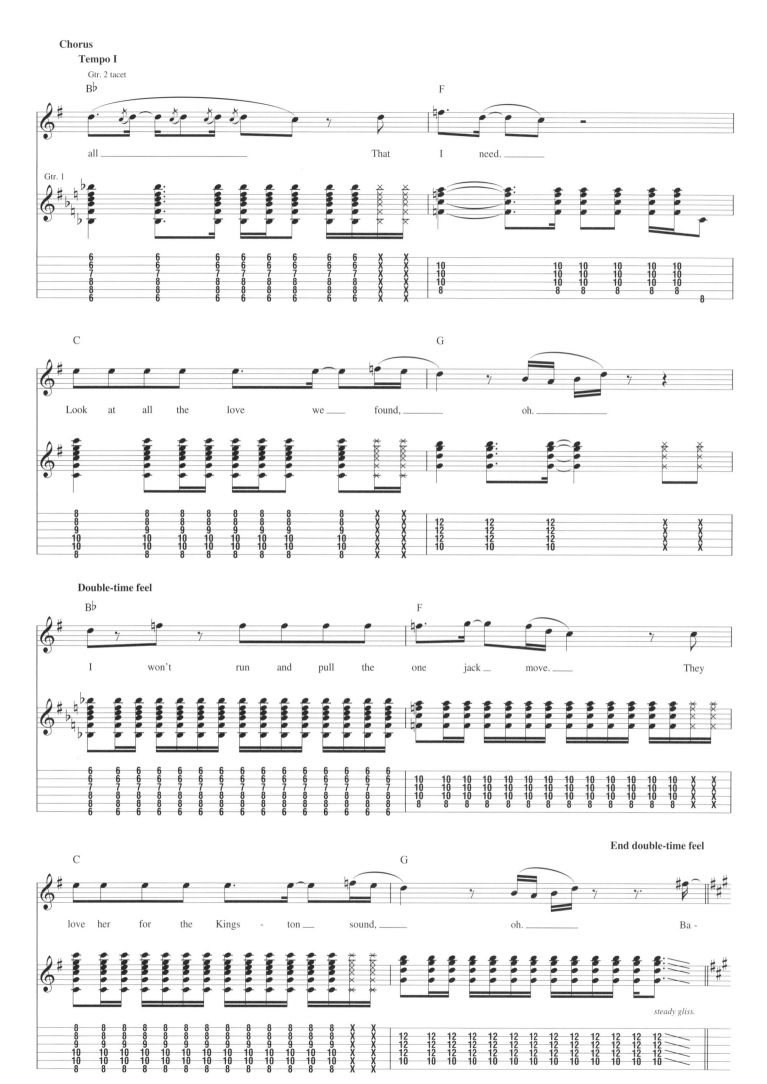

Outro

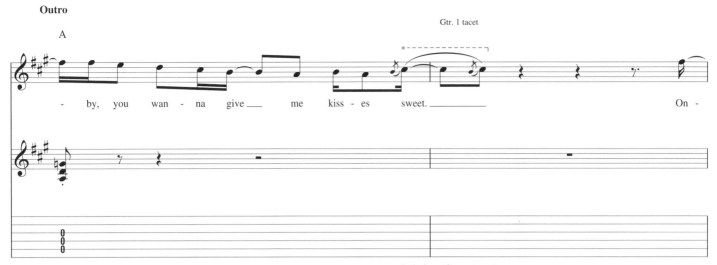

*w/ echo set for quarter-note
regeneration w/ 2 repeats

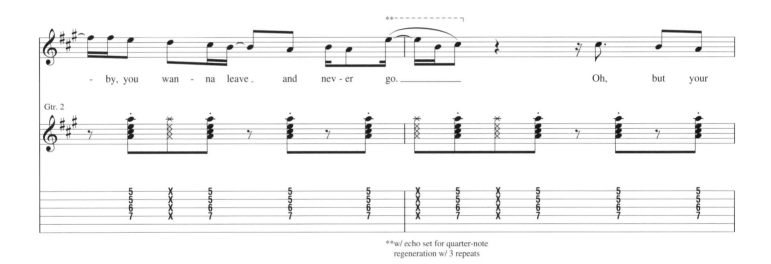

**w/ echo set for quarter-note
regeneration w/ 3 repeats

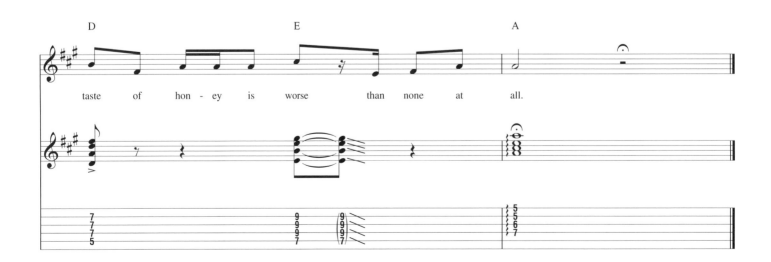

Boss D.J.

Words and Music by Brad Nowell

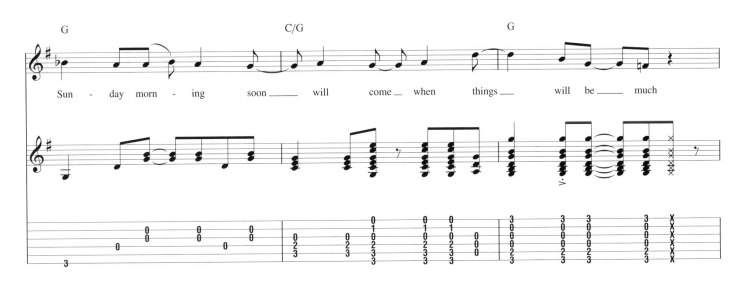

eas - i - er to say up - on the mi - cro - phone like a boss D. J. But I won't

walk up up - on the sea like it was dry land. __ The boss D. J., he ain't

noth - ing but a man. No trou - ble, no __ fuss. I __ know __ why. __

*Slap body of gtr. w/ right hand
in specified rhythm.

Chorus

Gtr. 1: w/ Rhy. Fig. 1 (2 times)

It's __ so __ nice. __ I wan - na __ hear the same song twice. __

It's __ so __ nice. __ I wan - na __ hear the same song twice. 2. Ru - mors are

Falling Idols

Words and Music by Randy Bradbury, Ross Fletcher, Greg Lowther, Willard Pangborn and David Quackenbush

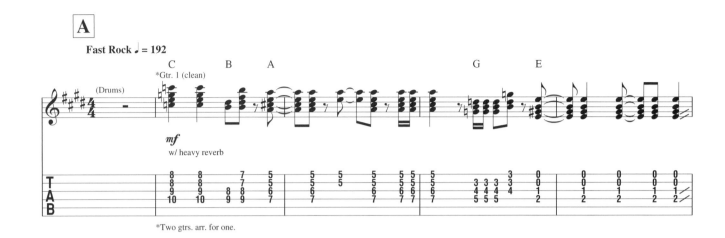

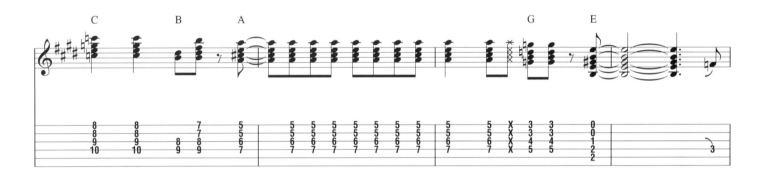

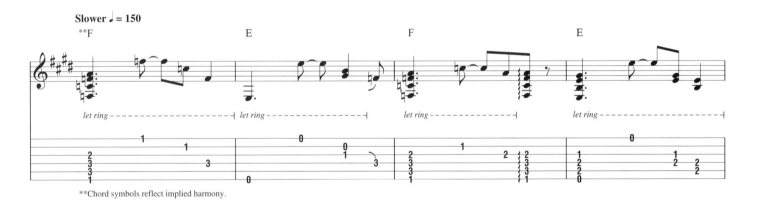

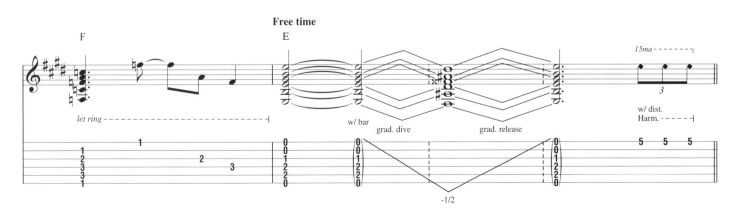

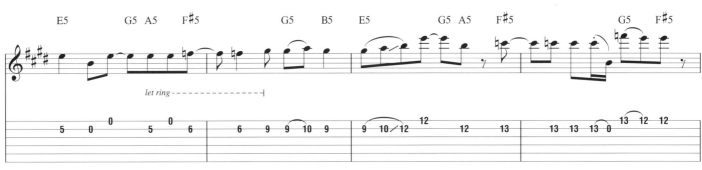

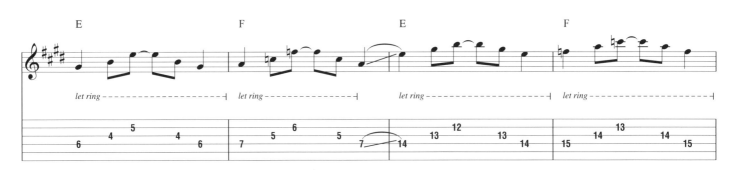

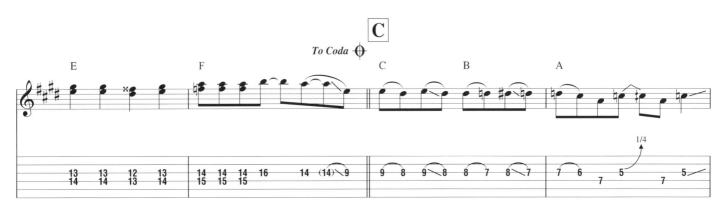

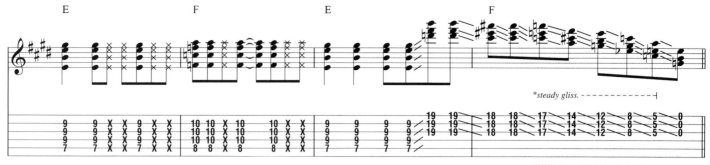

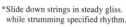

*Slide down strings in steady gliss.
while strumming specified rhythm.

E

F

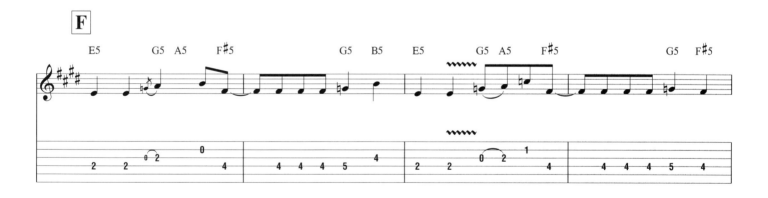

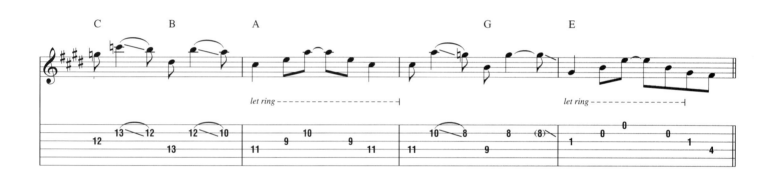

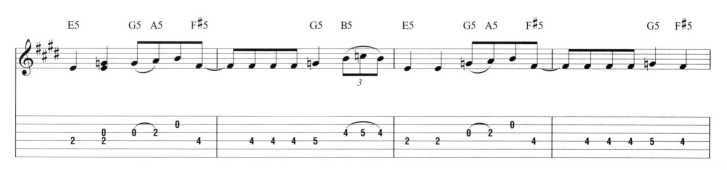

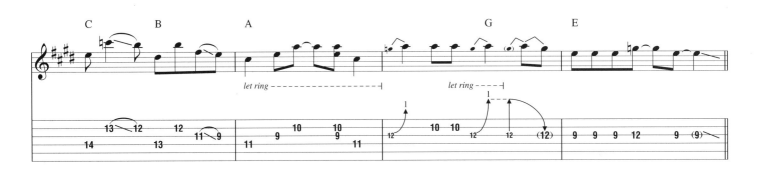

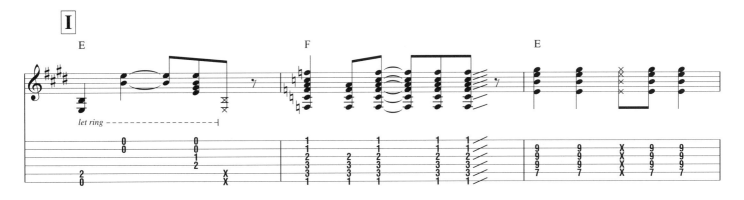

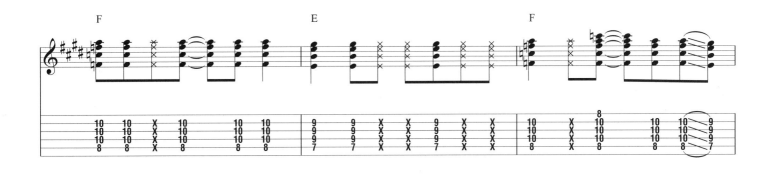

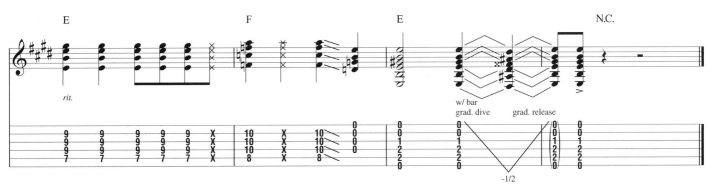

All You Need

Words and Music by Brad Nowell

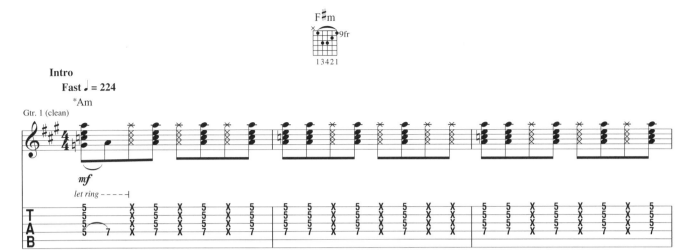

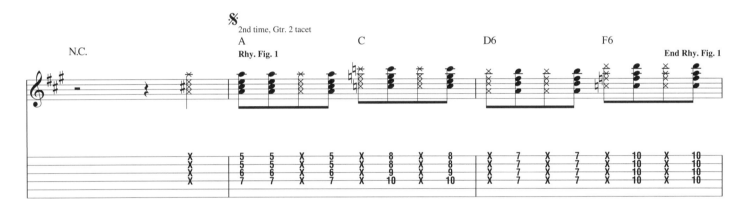

*Chord symbols reflect overall harmony.

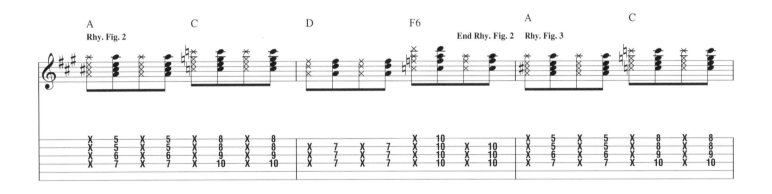

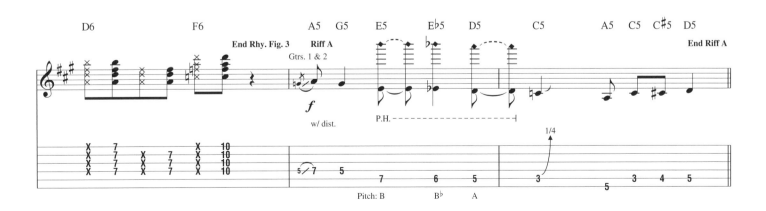

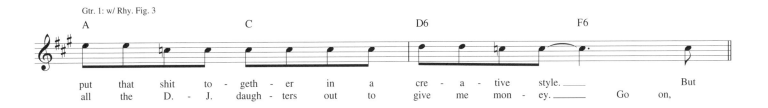

u - Roy style.__ We got to put that shit to - geth - er in a cre - a - tive style.__ We
love, love,__ love.__ And if I nev - er re - al - ize, then that's how it has to be. And

Gtr. 1: w/ Rhy. Fig. 3

put that shit to - geth - er in a cre - a - tive style._____ But
all the D. J. daugh - ters out to give me mon - ey._____ Go on,

Pre-Chorus

2nd time, Gtrs. 1 & 2: w/ Rhy. Fill 1 (4 times)

out - side on the pave - ment, I won't __ feel a - fraid. There's a
back out on the free - way, I won't __ feel the same.

Gtr. 1

let ring -

w/ slight dist.

Gtr. 2

mf

let ring - - - - - - - - - - - - - - - -

w/ slight dist.

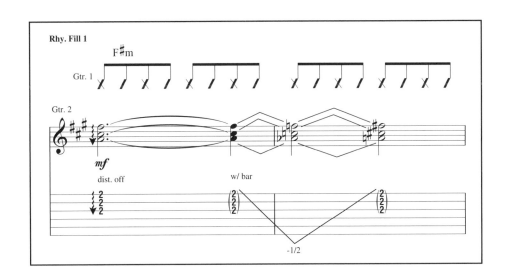

Rhy. Fill 1

F#m

Gtr. 1

Gtr. 2

mf

dist. off   w/ bar

-1/2

lit - tle piece of pa - per say - ing how we won't get paid.
Lit - tle yel - low head - lights look like snails smashed in the rain. ___

Chorus

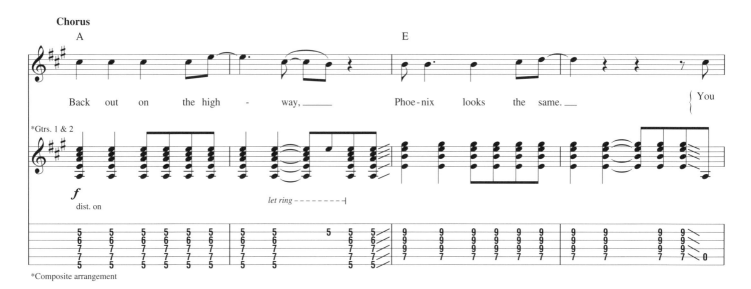

Back out on the high - way, ___ Phoe - nix looks the same. ___ You

*Gtrs. 1 & 2

*Composite arrangement

don't got me } 'cause I've got no one to blame. ___
Don't ask me }

⊕ Coda

Free time

That's all you nee - ee - eed. _____ Yeah. _____ Yeah. _____

Interlude

Tempo I

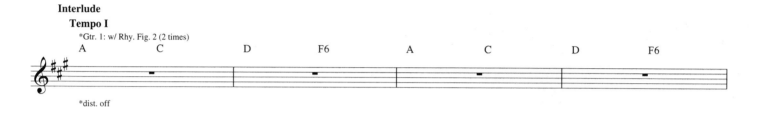

*Gtr. 1: w/ Rhy. Fig. 2 (2 times)

| A | C | D | F6 | A | C | D | F6 |

*dist. off

Gtr. 1: w/ Rhy. Fig. 3

Gtrs. 1 & 2: w/ Riff A

| A | C | D6 | F6 | A5 G5 | E5 | E♭5 | D5 | C5 | A5 C5 C♯5 D5 |

Guitar Solo

Slower ♩ = 100

Gtrs. 1 & 2 tacet

Gm

Gtr. 3 (dist.)

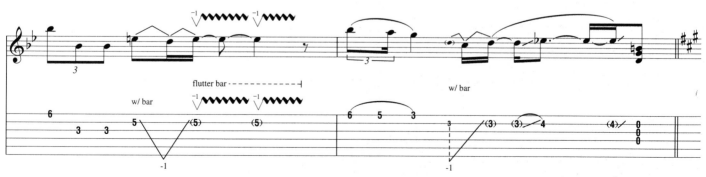

flutter bar - - - - - - - - - -

w/ bar

w/ bar

Real,
I want it real.

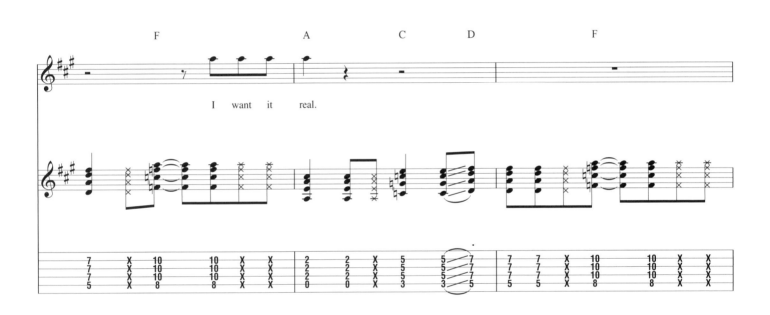

I want it real.

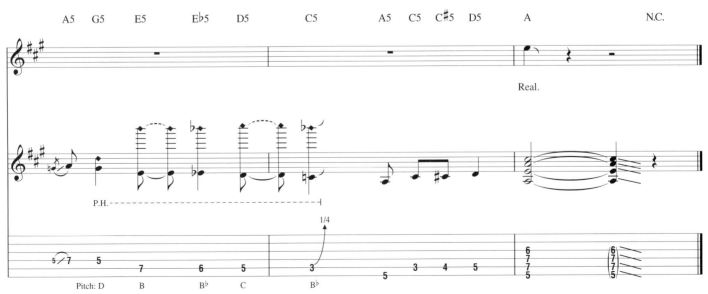

Real.

Freeway Time in LA County Jail

Words and Music by Brad Nowell

*Chord symbols reflect basic harmony.

1. On the freeway in the coun-ty, the sun don't shine.— I

feel, I feel, I feel, I feel a ba-ti man.— Out-side my cell dep-

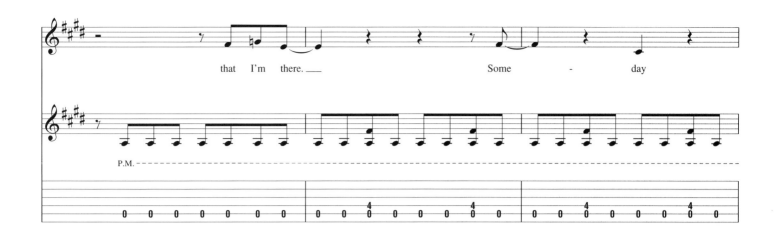

that I'm there. ___ Some - day

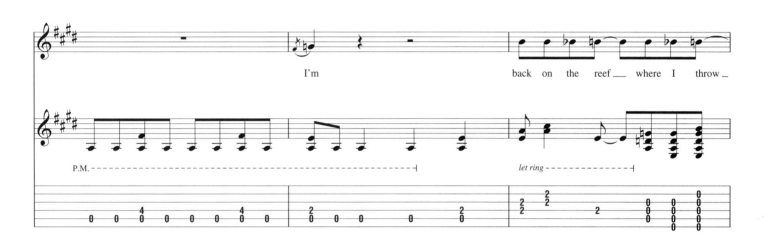

I'm back on the reef ___ where I throw ___

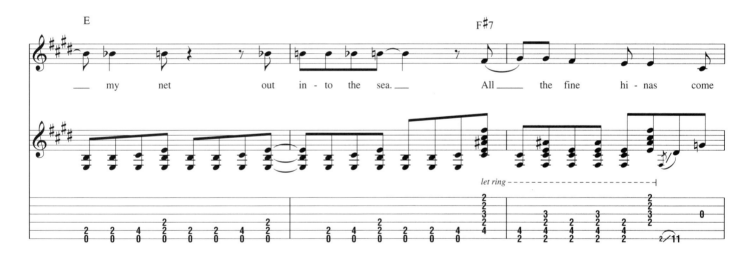

E   F#7

___ my net out in - to the sea. ___ All ___ the fine hi - nas come

Pre-Chorus

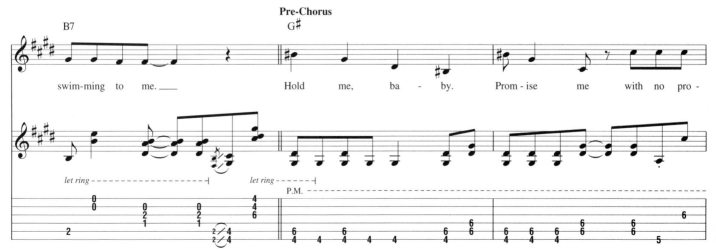

B7   G#

swim-ming to me. ___ Hold me, ba - by. Prom - ise me with no pro -

a wick - ed dog is a hun - gry dog. ____ I

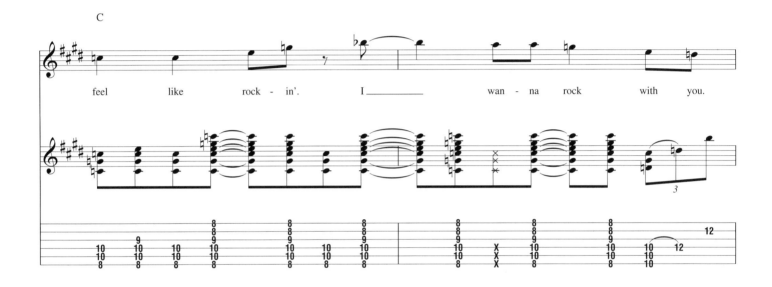

feel like rock - in'. I ____ wan - na rock with you.

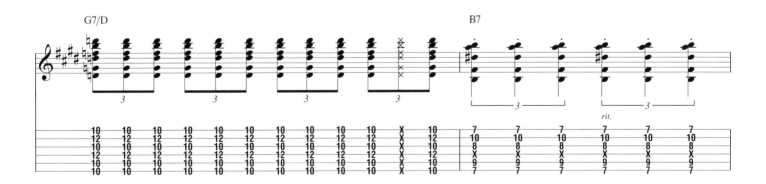

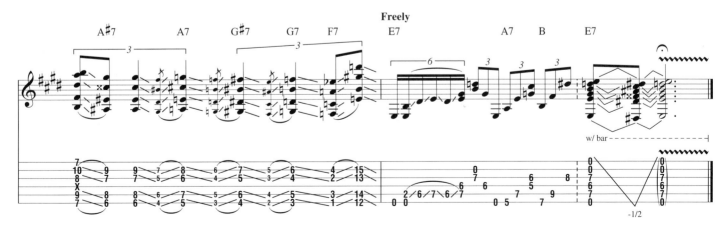

Mary

Words and Music by Brad Nowell

1. Ba - by, one breath a - way. I'll find the words to say.

*Chord symbols reflect implied harmony.

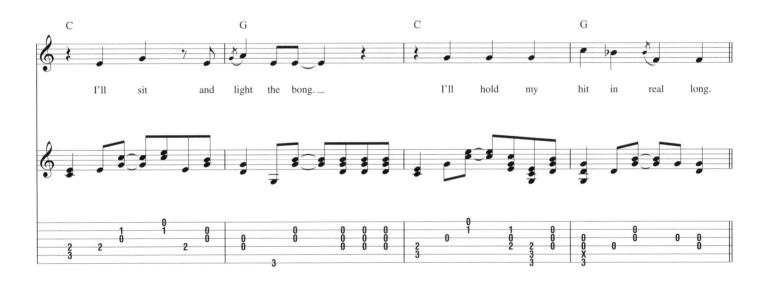

I'll sit and light the bong. I'll hold my hit in real long.

I don't know if I can go up in - side of you to - night.

Oh, Mar - y, ba - by, please ___ don't fuss and fight.

Verse

2. You've heard the line be - fore. ___ Mar - y, ba - by, please don't think I'm a bore. ___

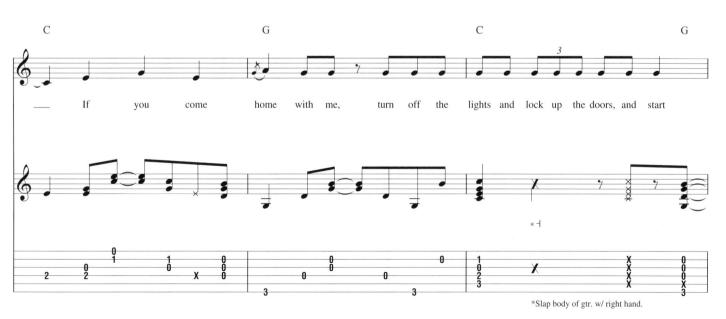

___ If you come home with me, turn off the lights and lock up the doors, and start

*Slap body of gtr. w/ right hand.

Chorus

get - ting bus - y. I don't know if I can ___ go so far up

in - side you to - night. ___ Oh, Mar - y, ba - by, I ___ could do it right.

Verse

3. When we got to the pad, ___ Mar - y, ba - by, start - ed call - in' me her dad. ___

Yes, she gave me head. __ We could not find the damn bed.

Chorus

Fif - teen years old plus __ one, hot - ter than __ a mi - cro - wave ov - en. __

__ Oh, Mar - y, ba - by, dad - dy is com - ing home.

Don't Push

Words and Music by Brad Nowell

Intro
Moderately slow ♩ = 86

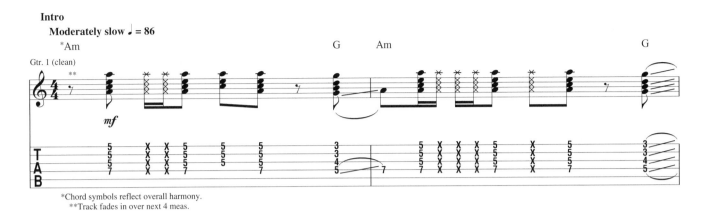

*Chord symbols reflect overall harmony.
**Track fades in over next 4 meas.

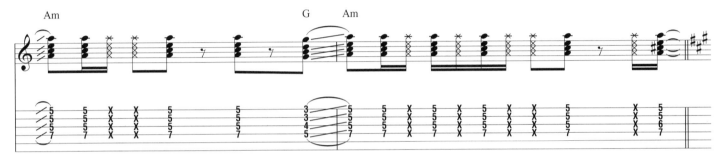

Verse

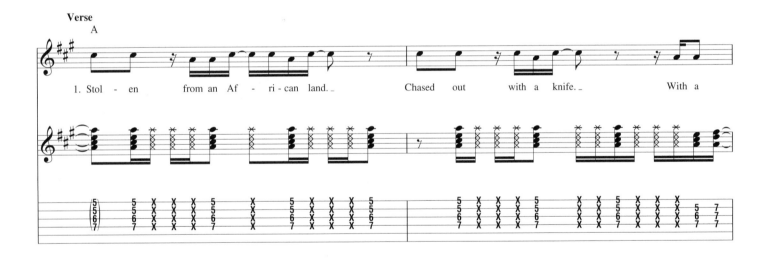

1. Stol - en   from an Af - ri - can land. ___   Chased   out   with a knife. ___   With a

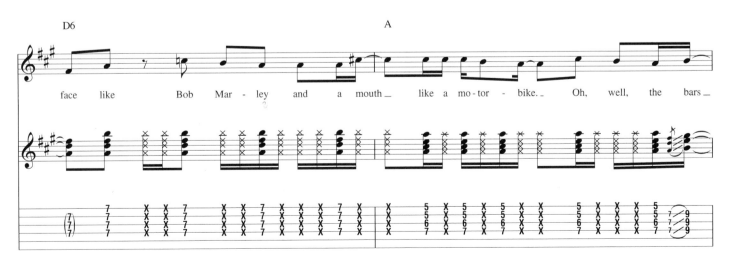

face   like   Bob   Mar - ley   and   a   mouth ___   like a mo - tor - bike.   Oh,   well,   the bars ___

*Bass plays E.

Bridge

88

*Bass plays E.

*Bass plays E.

Bridge

Verse

Laugh - ter, ___ it's free an - y - time just call me

four - three - eight - four - eight - three - six. This, the kind of num-ber make you get your kicks. Wah - da - bye!

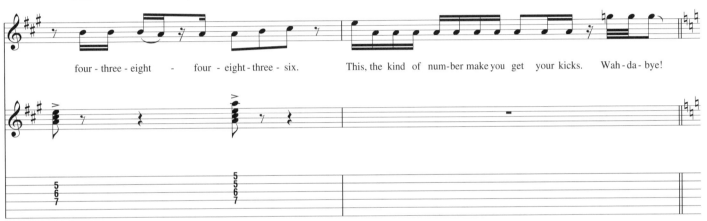

Outro

Begin fade

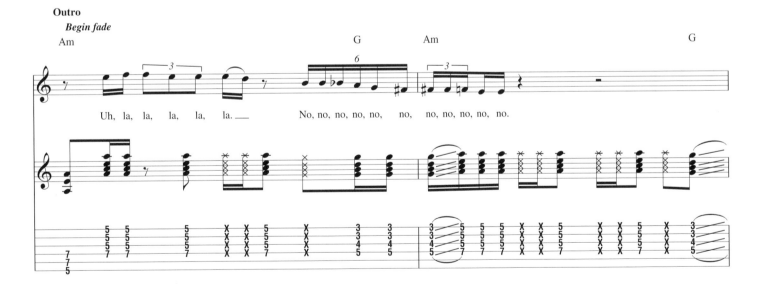

Uh, la, la, la, la, la. ___ No, no, no, no, no, no, no, no, no, no, no.

Fade out

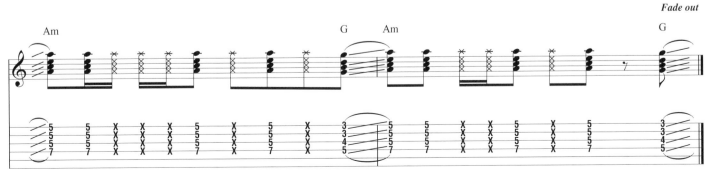

GUITAR NOTATION LEGEND

Guitar music can be notated three different ways: on a *musical staff*, in *tablature*, and in *rhythm slashes*.

RHYTHM SLASHES are written above the staff. Strum chords in the rhythm indicated. Use the chord diagrams found at the top of the first page of the transcription for the appropriate chord voicings. Round noteheads indicate single notes.

THE MUSICAL STAFF shows pitches and rhythms and is divided by bar lines into measures. Pitches are named after the first seven letters of the alphabet.

TABLATURE graphically represents the guitar fingerboard. Each horizontal line represents a string, and each number represents a fret.

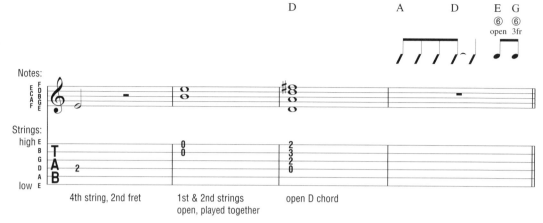

4th string, 2nd fret

1st & 2nd strings open, played together

open D chord

Definitions for Special Guitar Notation

HALF-STEP BEND: Strike the note and bend up 1/2 step.

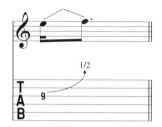

WHOLE-STEP BEND: Strike the note and bend up one step.

GRACE NOTE BEND: Strike the note and immediately bend up as indicated.

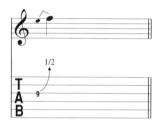

SLIGHT (MICROTONE) BEND: Strike the note and bend up 1/4 step.

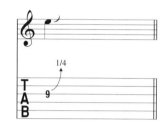

BEND AND RELEASE: Strike the note and bend up as indicated, then release back to the original note. Only the first note is struck.

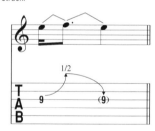

PRE-BEND: Bend the note as indicated, then strike it.

PRE-BEND AND RELEASE: Bend the note as indicated. Strike it and release the bend back to the original note.

UNISON BEND: Strike the two notes simultaneously and bend the lower note up to the pitch of the higher.

VIBRATO: The string is vibrated by rapidly bending and releasing the note with the fretting hand.

WIDE VIBRATO: The pitch is varied to a greater degree by vibrating with the fretting hand.

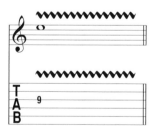

HAMMER-ON: Strike the first (lower) note with one finger, then sound the higher note (on the same string) with another finger by fretting it without picking.

PULL-OFF: Place both fingers on the notes to be sounded. Strike the first note and without picking, pull the finger off to sound the second (lower) note.

LEGATO SLIDE: Strike the first note and then slide the same fret-hand finger up or down to the second note. The second note is not struck.

SHIFT SLIDE: Same as legato slide, except the second note is struck.

TRILL: Very rapidly alternate between the notes indicated by continuously hammering on and pulling off.

TAPPING: Hammer ("tap") the fret indicated with the pick-hand index or middle finger and pull off to the note fretted by the fret hand.

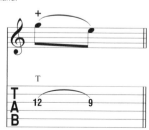

NATURAL HARMONIC: Strike the note while the fret-hand lightly touches the string directly over the fret indicated.

PINCH HARMONIC: The note is fretted normally and a harmonic is produced by adding the edge of the thumb or the tip of the index finger of the pick hand to the normal pick attack.

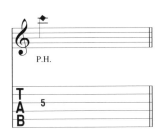

HARP HARMONIC: The note is fretted normally and a harmonic is produced by gently resting the pick hand's index finger directly above the indicated fret (in parentheses) while the pick hand's thumb or pick assists by plucking the appropriate string.

PICK SCRAPE: The edge of the pick is rubbed down (or up) the string, producing a scratchy sound.

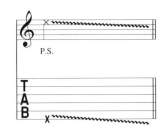

MUFFLED STRINGS: A percussive sound is produced by laying the fret hand across the string(s) without depressing, and striking them with the pick hand.

PALM MUTING: The note is partially muted by the pick hand lightly touching the string(s) just before the bridge.

RAKE: Drag the pick across the strings indicated with a single motion.

TREMOLO PICKING: The note is picked as rapidly and continuously as possible.

ARPEGGIATE: Play the notes of the chord indicated by quickly rolling them from bottom to top.

VIBRATO BAR DIVE AND RETURN: The pitch of the note or chord is dropped a specified number of steps (in rhythm), then returned to the original pitch.

VIBRATO BAR SCOOP: Depress the bar just before striking the note, then quickly release the bar.

VIBRATO BAR DIP: Strike the note and then immediately drop a specified number of steps, then release back to the original pitch.

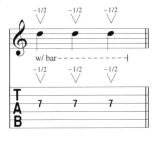

Additional Musical Definitions

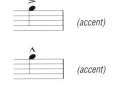	*(accent)*	• Accentuate note (play it louder).
	(accent)	• Accentuate note with great intensity.
	(staccato)	• Play the note short.
		• Downstroke
		• Upstroke
D.S. al Coda		• Go back to the sign (%), then play until the measure marked "***To Coda***," then skip to the section labelled "**Coda**."
D.C. al Fine		• Go back to the beginning of the song and play until the measure marked "***Fine***" (end).

Rhy. Fig.	• Label used to recall a recurring accompaniment pattern (usually chordal).
Riff	• Label used to recall composed, melodic lines (usually single notes) which recur.
Fill	• Label used to identify a brief melodic figure which is to be inserted into the arrangement.
Rhy. Fill	• A chordal version of a Fill.
tacet	• Instrument is silent (drops out).
	• Repeat measures between signs.
	• When a repeated section has different endings, play the first ending only the first time and the second ending only the second time.

NOTE: Tablature numbers in parentheses mean:
1. The note is being sustained over a system (note in standard notation is tied), or
2. The note is sustained, but a new articulation (such as a hammer-on, pull-off, slide or vibrato) begins, or
3. The note is a barely audible "ghost" note (note in standard notation is also in parentheses).

GUITAR RECORDED VERSIONS®

Guitar Recorded Versions® are note-for-note transcriptions of guitar music taken directly off recordings. This series, one of the most popular in print today, features some of the greatest guitar players and groups from blues and rock to country and jazz.

Guitar Recorded Versions are transcribed by the best transcribers in the business. Every book contains notes and tablature. Visit www.halleonard.com for our complete selection.

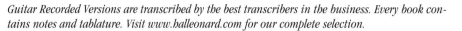

AUTHENTIC TRANSCRIPTIONS WITH NOTES AND TABLATURE

AUTHENTIC TRANSCRIPTIONS WITH NOTES AND TABLATURE

FOR MORE INFORMATION, SEE YOUR LOCAL MUSIC DEALER, OR WRITE TO:

7777 W. BLUEMOUND RD. P.O. BOX 13819 MILWAUKEE, WI 53213

Complete songlists and more at **www.halleonard.com**
Prices, contents, and availability subject to change without notice.

1110

GUITAR *signature licks*

Signature Licks book/CD packs provide a step-by-step breakdown of "right from the record" riffs, licks, and solos so you can jam along with your favorite bands. They contain performance notes and an overview of each artist's or group's style, with note-for-note transcriptions in notes and tab. The CDs feature full-band demos at both normal and slow speeds.

ACOUSTIC CLASSICS
00695864 ....$19.95

AEROSMITH 1973-1979
00695106 ....$22.95

AEROSMITH 1979-1998
00695219 ....$22.95

BEST OF AGGRO-METAL
00695592 ....$19.95

DUANE ALLMAN
00696042 ....$22.95

BEST OF CHET ATKINS
00695752 ....$22.95

THE BEACH BOYS DEFINITIVE COLLECTION
00695683 ....$22.95

BEST OF THE BEATLES FOR ACOUSTIC GUITAR
00695453 ....$22.95

THE BEATLES BASS
00695283 ....$22.95

THE BEATLES FAVORITES
00695096 ....$24.95

THE BEATLES HITS
00695049 ....$24.95

BEST OF GEORGE BENSON
00695418 ....$22.95

BEST OF BLACK SABBATH
00695249 ....$22.95

BEST OF BLINK - 182
00695704 ....$22.95

BEST OF BLUES GUITAR
00695846 ....$19.95

BLUES GUITAR CLASSICS
00695177 ....$19.95

BLUES/ROCK GUITAR MASTERS
00695348 ....$21.95

KENNY BURRELL
00695830 ....$22.99

BEST OF CHARLIE CHRISTIAN
00695584 ....$22.95

BEST OF ERIC CLAPTON
00695038 ....$24.95

ERIC CLAPTON – THE BLUESMAN
00695040 ....$22.95

ERIC CLAPTON – FROM THE ALBUM UNPLUGGED
00695250 ....$24.95

BEST OF CREAM
00695251 ....$22.95

CREEDANCE CLEARWATER REVIVAL
00695924 ....$22.95

DEEP PURPLE – GREATEST HITS
00695625 ....$22.95

THE BEST OF DEF LEPPARD
00696516 ....$22.95

THE DOORS
00695373 ....$22.95

ESSENTIAL JAZZ GUITAR
00695875 ....$19.99

FAMOUS ROCK GUITAR SOLOS
00695590 ....$19.95

BEST OF FOO FIGHTERS
00695481 ....$24.95

ROBBEN FORD
00695903 ....$22.95

GREATEST GUITAR SOLOS OF ALL TIME
00695301 ....$19.95

BEST OF GRANT GREEN
00695747 ....$22.95

BEST OF GUNS N' ROSES
00695183 ....$24.95

THE BEST OF BUDDY GUY
00695186 ....$22.95

JIM HALL
00695848 ....$22.99

HARD ROCK SOLOS
00695591 ....$19.95

JIMI HENDRIX
00696560 ....$24.95

JIMI HENDRIX – VOLUME 2
00695835 ....$24.95

JOHN LEE HOOKER
00695894 ....$19.99

HOT COUNTRY GUITAR
00695580 ....$19.95

BEST OF JAZZ GUITAR
00695586 ....$24.95

ERIC JOHNSON
00699317 ....$24.95

ROBERT JOHNSON
00695264 ....$22.95

BARNEY KESSEL
00696009 ....$22.99

THE ESSENTIAL ALBERT KING
00695713 ....$22.95

B.B. KING – THE DEFINITIVE COLLECTION
00695635 ....$22.95

B.B. KING – MASTER BLUESMAN
00699923 ....$24.99

THE KINKS
00695553 ....$22.95

BEST OF KISS
00699413 ....$22.95

MARK KNOPFLER
00695178 ....$22.95

LYNYRD SKYNYRD
00695872 ....$24.95

BEST OF YNGWIE MALMSTEEN
00695669 ....$22.95

BEST OF PAT MARTINO
00695632 ....$24.99

WES MONTGOMERY
00695387 ....$24.95

BEST OF NIRVANA
00695483 ....$24.95

THE OFFSPRING
00695852 ....$24.95

VERY BEST OF OZZY OSBOURNE
00695431 ....$22.95

BEST OF JOE PASS
00695730 ....$22.95

TOM PETTY
00696021 ....$22.99

PINK FLOYD – EARLY CLASSICS
00695566 ....$22.95

THE POLICE
00695724 ....$22.95

THE GUITARS OF ELVIS
00696507 ....$22.95

BEST OF QUEEN
00695097 ....$24.95

BEST OF RAGE AGAINST THE MACHINE
00695480 ....$24.95

RED HOT CHILI PEPPERS
00695173 ....$22.95

RED HOT CHILI PEPPERS – GREATEST HITS
00695828 ....$24.95

BEST OF DJANGO REINHARDT
00695660 ....$24.95

BEST OF ROCK
00695884 ....$19.95

BEST OF ROCK 'N' ROLL GUITAR
00695559 ....$19.95

BEST OF ROCKABILLY GUITAR
00695785 ....$19.95

THE ROLLING STONES
00695079 ....$24.95

BEST OF DAVID LEE ROTH
00695843 ....$24.95

BEST OF JOE SATRIANI
00695216 ....$22.95

BEST OF SILVERCHAIR
00695488 ....$22.95

THE BEST OF SOUL GUITAR
00695703 ....$19.95

BEST OF SOUTHERN ROCK
00695560 ....$19.95

MIKE STERN
00695800 ....$24.99

ROD STEWART
00695663 ....$22.95

BEST OF SURF GUITAR
00695822 ....$19.95

BEST OF SYSTEM OF A DOWN
00695788 ....$22.95

ROCK BAND
00696063 ....$22.99

ROBIN TROWER
00695950 ....$22.95

STEVE VAI
00673247 ....$22.95

STEVE VAI – ALIEN LOVE SECRETS: THE NAKED VAMPS
00695223 ....$22.95

STEVE VAI – FIRE GARDEN: THE NAKED VAMPS
00695166 ....$22.95

STEVE VAI – THE ULTRA ZONE: NAKED VAMPS
00695684 ....$22.95

STEVIE RAY VAUGHAN – 2ND ED.
00699316 ....$24.95

THE GUITAR STYLE OF STEVIE RAY VAUGHAN
00695155 ....$24.95

BEST OF THE VENTURES
00695772 ....$19.95

THE WHO – 2ND ED.
00695561 ....$22.95

JOHNNY WINTER
00695951 ....$22.99

BEST OF ZZ TOP
00695738 ....$24.95

FOR MORE INFORMATION,
SEE YOUR LOCAL MUSIC DEALER,
OR WRITE TO:

HAL•LEONARD®
CORPORATION
7777 W. BLUEMOUND RD. P.O. BOX 13819
MILWAUKEE, WISCONSIN 53213

www.halleonard.com

COMPLETE DESCRIPTIONS AND SONGLISTS ONLINE!
Prices, contents and availability subject to change without notice.

0410